Emma Brewer

Precious Stones

their homes, histories, and influence

Emma Brewer

Precious Stones
their homes, histories, and influence

ISBN/EAN: 9783337300111

Printed in Europe, USA, Canada, Australia, Japan

Cover: Foto ©Andreas Hilbeck / pixelio.de

More available books at **www.hansebooks.com**

THE GIRL'S OWN ANNUAL

XV.

Illustrated.

LONDON: 56, PATERNOSTER ROW.

THE GIRL'S OWN PAPER

Vol. XV.—No. 721.]   OCTOBER 21, 1893.   [Price One Penny.

MERMAIDENS.

By SARAH TYTLER, Author of "A Young Oxford Maid," etc.

THE THREE SISTERS.   (*From a miniature.*)

CHAPTER III.

MORE OF OURSELVES.

SALLY was four years my senior, and was in her seventeenth year at the date to which I am referring. She was just casting the last traces of her childhood behind her. Being the eldest of the family, and precocious, she had discarded her dolls years before she was in her teens. She had since done the same with her fairy-tales, her ball, and her skipping-rope. She was a well-grown girl, and Aunt Maria, who presided like an absolute sovereign, without a notion of rebellion on our part, over the different stages of our youth, had put Sally into long frocks. Aunt Maria had also decreed that Sally should turn up her hair, and fasten it on the top of her head with a high comb, so that she looked inches taller than she had done the week before in her short frocks with her hair on her shoulders. The promotion turned Sally's head a little; she not only left childish things behind her, she gave herself airs, we younger ones thought; and it was only her kindness of heart which prevented her from having anything to do with us. She sat a great deal with Aunt Maria, stitching demurely in her company, though Sally had detested needle-work formerly, and she had always been the foremost in stealing up on deck and playing hide-and-seek on the different decks and round the masts. Indeed, it had been her greatest grief that she was not allowed to climb a mast as Tom and the other boys went aloft. I believe she would have attempted it privately had she not stood in some awe of the captain of the main-topmast, who was continually telling us what was and was not proper for young misses to do. Now she sailed languidly along the deck, and as to entering the cockpit, she would have scorned anything so far beneath her years and her dignity, though I am sure she hankered after the joyous games of "Blind-man's-buff" and "I spy" we had without her. She spoke to Mr. Rhodes, the chaplain who taught us, as if she were on an equality with him; and strange to say he accepted the equality, though it was only the other day that he had rated her soundly for mistakes in her grammar and spelling. She did not so much as let her eyes rest on the sailing-master, though not three months ago she had wheedled him into including her in the special lessons in navigation which he was giving Tom and cousin Perry. When our Sally expected to sail a ship, to conduct its signals, to steer it clear of one enemy and to bring it to bear on another, was more than she herself could have told.

But Sally in her new and exalted estate was hardest of all on our relative Perry Hood. He was older than Tom, about Sally's own age—a little spare, freckled boy, thoughtful, unselfish, and fond of us all, so that we were fond of him in return. Sally had been the

fondest, and the two had been the greatest friends in the world; but after she blossomed into a young lady she would hardly notice him. She paid not the slightest attention to his finest feats in running out to the ends of the yards and standing waving his cap at the very top of the mizzen-mast, of which he made a desperate display in the vain hope of recovering her good graces. She treated him with the greatest coldness and superciliousness, so that the poor fellow was baffled and hurt by the unaccounted-for breach in their friendship. We, his allies, were furious with Sally for her fickleness and arrogance.

A sister does not, as a rule, form any very lively or correct estimate of a sister's looks—good, bad, or indifferent. But when I try to see across the gulf of years behind me, I come to the conclusion that our Sally must have grown up rather a fine-looking girl. She was not a pink-and-white drawing-room belle, she was always a little brown with sun and wind, but she had the unapproachable carriage, at once erect and supple, of a right royal queen who is supposed to carry her crown poised on her head, or of a vigorous independent fish-wife, who really bears her "creel" of fish strapped between her shoulders. She had steel-blue eyes which could flash and sparkle under their brown lashes, and a quantity of light brown hair, weighing heavily on that aspiring comb of hers which did its tucking-up with an effort. People said Sally was like our mother with a super-added dash of father and Aunt Maria in their strong-mindedness and determination.

Tom resembled father and Aunt Maria in face and figure, but it was the two with a difference. His dark grey eyes were so merry, and the teeth which represented their broken and dilapidated sets so glancing in their whiteness, that they quite lit up his dark face. He never looked as if he had swallowed a ramrod or a poker, as truth compels me to own his worthy seniors sometimes looked. He was a dear, good boy on the whole, though his high spirits and hot temper occasionally got him into scrapes, and whoever father spared, he could not spare Tom, because the admiral's son must always be an example of one kind or another. He was the life of the family as well as of the ship. Father would screw up his mouth and Aunt Maria would knit her forehead to save them from exploding with laughter at some of Tom's odd fancies and droll sayings. We all knew that when Tom was posted as lieutenant, if he chanced to be appointed to another ship, a casualty which father might use his interest to bring about, as better for Tom, we should be dreadfully dull, even at sea, without him.

Jane was next to Tom. Poor little Jane! Whether from innate delicacy of constitution, or, as Aunt Maria was strongly inclined to hold, from a concealed fall, to which a careless nurse had subjected her when she was a baby, Jane was not like the rest of us. She was a puny creature, with a suspicion of deformity about her large head and narrow sloping shoulders. Neither sun

nor wind brought a fresh colour or even a healthful brownness into her small, sallow face. She had pretty brown eyes; but they looked out pathetically from the hollow caverns in which they were sunk. There was no gold or tawny auburn in the brown of her hair. It had a dead flaxen under-tint, as if it had ashes for its foundation. She was so slight and thin that her wrists and ankles were like the spindle-shanks of a sickly child. But if Jane had the smallest, weakest body, she had the biggest soul among us. She was by far the cleverest of the family. At her urgent entreaty, the chaplain taught her Greek and Latin, which he said she learnt with ease. She read greedily every book she could get her hands upon, from *Hervey's Meditations among the Tombs*, and Virgil's *Georgics* and *Bucolics*, to the essays and stories in the *Ladies' Magazine*—which Aunt Maria took out—when she could get the numbers, and Tabitha Tidy's Hints on General Neatness for the Benefit of Young Gentlewomen.

At intervals father and Aunt Maria held serious consultations on sending Jane to live on shore with some distant relations of mother's. This was not that she might receive a higher and more thorough education, which by cultivating her remarkable abilities might have afforded her compensation for the penalties of a feeble body and a person worn and overshadowed by sickness. Such compensations were not thought of in those days. A boy or a girl had to accept his or her fate and make the best of it, bowing to the will of Providence. The proposal was made under the impression that the life at sea, on which the rest of us flourished, might be too hard for Jane's weakly constitution, and that she would receive more medical solace and a greater choice of medical aid on shore. But Jane herself resisted the proposal strenuously. She cried bitterly when she was a child at the idea of being parted from us. After she was older she fretted unmistakably over the plan. As a consequence of this passive opposition, the scheme, once or twice taken up, was always abandoned in the end.

Apart from this bone of contention Jane was wonderfully contented under her deprivations and sufferings, for she had many a sharp tussle with pain and weariness, which she bore for the most part uncomplainingly, with the touching patience and fortitude which one sometimes sees in a very baby. She was accustomed to carry her burden, and her back was made for it. She was no fool, young as she was, to fight aimlessly with her destiny, and good principles of faith and submission had been early instilled into her. She found innumerable subjects to interest her beyond what we shared. She was always busy in her way, unless when she had her bouts of disabling illness, with her books and her drawing. She had got occasional lessons in drawing when we were in port, and she had improved on them, till she was a fair draughtswoman. Every visit to a new place, every unconventional face or figure she encountered afforded scope for this talent. She had her collections of shells and of botanical and entomological specimens, to which she was always adding. Her brother and sisters were ignoramuses and numbsculls beside Jane, although she always made light of what desultory information she had acquired, and thirsted for deeper and more thorough knowledge. She was normally contented and as cheerful as any of us ; when she did fret it was largely in response to Aunt Maria's fretting on her account. For unfortunately Aunt Maria could not witness Jane's infirmities without yielding to the impression that somebody was to blame for them. Either she herself had neglected precautions which would have prevented the mischief, or Jane had been, or was at the present moment, guilty of some rashness, the effect of which formed the root of her malady. Aunt Maria worried both herself and Jane on this head, until many a time Jane would be driven to cry out, " Oh, if Aunt Maria would only let me alone ! If she could but be brought to look to

first causes ! If she would acknowledge practically that whatever laws may or may not be broken, it is really God's will that some of us should be crooked and some of us straight, some of us strong and some of us weak. Everything would be so much easier to bear if she would see it in that light." This struggle did not interfere with the strong regard which existed between Aunt Maria and Jane ; indeed, I believe Jane's vexation was induced by the sense that she could not satisfy Aunt Maria. There was a still deeper attachment between father and Jane, expressed in the quietest manner.

I was Caroline, the youngest, " Caroline " only to father and Aunt Maria, " Car " to Tom, Sally and Jane, to Cousin Perry and to our particular friends among the young officers. They all said I was like both Sally and Tom. I was a big girl for my years, as Sally was for hers, and I had her hair and complexion, but I had Tom's and my father's dark grey eyes, and I had Tom's mouth and teeth—smaller because I was a girl-- I had the very dimple in his cheek,

which, to be sure, was rather girlish in a boy. (He was very much ashamed of it, and he would puff out his chubby cheeks to try to hide it.) I was healthy and hardy, for which I was even then thankful, though Aunt Maria was tempted to grudge the surplus health which I could not transfer to Jane, and to say it made me a tomboy. I do not think it was that, so much as the fact that Sally's being grown up, as she fondly imagined, and Jane being *hors de combat* and living in a world of her own—made up of books and drawing-copies and what Tom called her " logical specimens," which I had not the wit and taste to enter, I was thrown back for companionship, especially in play hours, on Tom and the middies nearest my age. After all, though they helped me to tear my frocks, dirty my hands, and make what Aunt Maria called " a furze bush " of my hair, and though they taught me to play " Rounds " and " Fives " and other games, not usually included in a girl's education, I cannot recall that they taught me anything worse.

(*To be continued.*)

ANGELS' FOOD.

By DORA DE BLAQUIÈRE.

CAKE—or, perhaps, as it would be better called, the sweetmeat —known today under the name of " angels' food," is by no means of modern origin. Indeed, the basis of the mixture may be found as far back as the days of Queen Elizabeth, when a very light, porous kind of sweetmeat was made, in a rather more clumsy mode of manufacture, under the name of " angelic sweetmeat." The foundation of all " angel " cakes is much the same, the chief distinction between them consisting in the number of eggs used, which varies from eight to one dozen. Nor need the housekeeper, who is anxious to make the attempt to manufacture " angel cake " of any kind, be deterred by the seeming expense, for there are plenty of good eggs to be obtained, bailing from " foreign parts "—from Normandy, Brittany, or Holland—at the comparatively small price of thirteen at a shilling, and in the summer time even less.

The first recipe I shall give is quite a new one, and hails from America ; it is called " angels' food " : — 1½ cups of pulverised (castor) sugar ; 1 cupful of flour ; 1 teaspoonful of cream of tartar ; the whites of ten eggs beaten to a stiff froth.

The newest English-American recipe I can find differs but little from it, and is as follows :—The whites of eleven eggs which have been kept in a very cool place, or upon ice, before they are used ; one tumbler and a half of castor sugar ; three-fourths of a tumbler of flour ; one level teaspoonful of cream of tartar, and one teaspoonful of flavouring—almond,

lemon, or vanilla, whichever is preferred— lemon being the best, I think, of all.

The following instructions for making should be strictly followed :—The ingredients should be all carefully gathered together before their blending, that they may be all to hand conveniently. Mix the cream of tartar and the flour together and sift the mixture several times, adding a small pinch of salt. Beat the eggs (whites only) to a very stiff froth, and add the sugar to it very quickly and quietly ; then, when these are well mixed, put in the flour in the same manner, sprinkling both through your fingers and being careful to avoid any lumps of either. One of the secrets of making " angel cake " is the method of mixing it. You do not exactly either beat it or stir it, but you lift it up and down with your fork from the bottom of the tin ; and if the first cake should turn out either tough or sticky, you will know that your mixing has been too violent, and with your next you must be more gentle. Put your cake into a clean, bright cake-tin (and some good authorities will tell you on no account to butter it) ; the oven should be a cool one, or, at least very moderate, and you may bake for forty-five minutes. Wait a quarter of an hour before you look at it, and be careful not to keep the oven-door open too long. You can try the cake with a straw to see if it be done. Many people cool this cake off by leaving the oven-door open and allowing it to remain for a time, and then taking it out and standing it upon the table to cool off. Before putting it into the oven you should sprinkle the top lightly with powdered sugar, but not so much sugar should be used as would make the cake fall in baking it.

Amongst the varieties of angels' food which are indulged in in America, are " angel surprise cake," " almond angel cake," " angel custards," and angels' cake made with peaches, bananas, and pineapples. The first named " surprise cake " is made with a freshly-made angel's cake, which for this purpose should

be baked in a round tin, and left in the tin until it be quite cold. When turned out, the first thing to do is to cut off the top, about half an inch thick, then take a sharp knife and cut round the inside of the cake, about half an inch from the crust, or the outer wall of the cake, and so take out the soft white centre. Then to whip a pint of fresh cream into a stiff froth and flavour with vanilla or lemon ; pour it into the hollow cake and smooth it over the top so that you can replace the lid, and make it look as if it were quite undisturbed. This, of course, constitutes the " surprise " when cut. Many people add candied fruit or almonds to the cream.

" Almond angel cake " is also a delicious confection made in much the same manner as the preceding, except that the cake is cut in layers, and the whipped cream is mixed with half a pound of almonds, blanched, and cut in small pieces. The cream is then put in between the layers, and the top is cut open, so as to allow the cream to be the top layer ; and some of the almonds, cut into long and thin pieces, are stuck into it ; so as to make it look " porcupiny." " Angel custards" are made in rather a different manner, for the angel batter must be baked in muffin rings, and, as usual, the cakes when baked must be left to get perfectly cold before being turned out. Then the top must be cut off each cake, and some of the inside taken off, which you must replace with a custard, which you may make as rich, or as simple, as you please. The following is a cheap and good recipe for a custard, which you may use with angel cake, or in any other way. Take the yolks of two eggs, a tumbler of milk, and four lumps of sugar. Simmer till thick, stirring the mixture carefully to prevent burning. Add a few drops of vanilla flavouring, and pour into a clean jug. Stir till cold.

I have left the preparation of " angel fruit cakes " until the last. They are nearly all made in the same way, namely, the angel batter, instead of being baked in only one cake, is baked in layers in the small round tins to be purchased at any tinsmith's, made for that purpose. They must not be very brown nor burnt. The lower layer of all must be spread with whipped, sweetened, and flavoured cream, and then you should cover this with a layer of bananas, peeled, and daintily sliced. Then put on another layer of cake, and repeat the addition of cream, and the sliced bananas. There are generally three layers of cake used, the top layer being completely covered up with the whipped cream.

Angel peach and pineapple cakes are made in the same manner, and both can be made of the preserved or canned fruits instead of the fresh, and so are suitable for winter as well as for summer use.

And no account of angels' food would be quite complete unless it were supplemented by a mention and a recipe for "angel water," called in French *Eau d'Ange*. This is of very ancient use in England, and is often spoken of during the time of the plague. It was also called "Portugal water," and was in great repute at one time for its healing properties. Simple "angel water" is made of the flowering tops of the myrtle only, distilled with water; but there are three or four kinds of aromatic waters, under the same name, that contain many more ingredients, and are known under the various names of "distilled musk" and "boiled angel water." In a very old cookery-book in my possession there are at least half a dozen recipes for "angel water." A simple one, that could be made at home, was—1 pint of orange-flower water, 1 pint of rose-water, and ½ pint of "myrtle-water;" to these put ¼ ounce of essence of musk, and 1 ounce of essence of ambergris; shake the whole together. This recipe is marked "to be made in small quantities only, soon spoiled, either by heat or cold."

I find a recipe for distilled "angel water" is made thus:—Gum benzoine (crushed small), 4 ounces; liquid styrax, 2 ounces; cloves (bruised), ½ ounce; Calamus aromaticus (bruised), ¼ ounce; cinnamon (bruised), ¼ ounce; coriander-seed (bruised), 1 drachm; water, 7 pints; distil ½ gallon.

We have left off the home manufacture of all these fragrant waters, which used to form a great part of the duties of our ancestresses. The "still-room maid" retains her name, but has other duties to perform, and the recipes are shut up in mouldy and unused books. But I am sure much of the beauty of our lives went out with these old avocations and fashions; and in order to regain something lost we shall have to make our tastes more simple, and go back to that almost forgotten love of the country, its quiet and peace, away from the hurried and unrestful life of the great city.

PRECIOUS STONES; THEIR HOMES, HISTORIES, AND INFLUENCE.

By EMMA BREWER.

INTRODUCTION.

"Dumb jewels often in their silent kind
More than quick words do move a woman's mind."—*Two Gentlemen of Verona.*

Of the many exquisite things nature turns out from her laboratories, precious stones carry away the palm both for beauty and fascination.

The mystery of their origin, the peculiarities of their native homes, their special characteristics, their medicinal qualities, their rarity and great value, the romances and tragedies in which they have played conspicuous parts, together with their marked influence on the lives of individuals and nations intensify our interest in them and sharpen our curiosity concerning them.

Beautiful and wonderful specimens as they are of nature's handiwork, they do not as a rule shine in all their splendour until they have passed through the hands of man; but this we shall see for ourselves as we follow each gem from its ancient home until, in its perfection, it adds fresh grace and beauty to the persons of the rich and the great.

All through the ages the method adopted by nature to form and perfect these gems has been enveloped in mystery, and, notwithstanding the intellect and knowledge which have been brought to bear upon this subject by successive generations, nature still manages to baffle us, and she has evidently no intention of gratifying our curiosity as to her process of manufacture.

One or two facts, however, the genius of man has wrested from her, for example, that she carries on her work in a particular class of rock and mountain, and that the materials she uses are quite of a common kind such as carbon, alumina, clay, and silica, with which we are all acquainted. A French scientist, Mons. Babinet, noting this fact, says, "It would seem as though the mighty creative and organising Power had chosen to manifest its omnipotence by producing the most valuable substances from the most ordinary elements."

But, when we come to the detail of nature's work, we are brought to a standstill, for she has not yet informed us how she brought together the elements of the stones, nor how she solidified the liquid or vaporous matters, for they could not have amalgamated in a solid state, nor even in a powdered form. Scientific men believe that she employed one of three means—volcanic heat and pressure, the aid of foreign material to dissolve the solution, or the slow decomposition of vegetable matter, but which they cannot decide. Nor do we know how long she takes to form and complete these gems.

One thing, however, is quite evident, *viz.*, that no workshop on the earth's surface has ever produced such treasures as the laboratories beneath it.

Pliny said "that in gems we have all the majesty of nature gathered in a small compass, and that in no other of her works has nature produced anything so admirable." Yet considering her boundless wealth of material and working power, it is surprising how small a number of precious stones have found their way into the world. Of course there may be many waiting and in readiness to be discovered, either by the skill of man, or by the freaks of their "Mother Nature," for her method of dealing with them is often curious. She produces them with the utmost care, sparing neither skill nor time to render them the most perfect of her treasures, and, when at length there is nothing more to desire, she wraps them round with quite common garments, which hide from view their exquisite form and colour, and with scant courtesy starts them on their career.

Not till the hand of man has touched them, and with skill removed their coverings do they stand forth in the light pure, transparent, splendid, fit emblems of all heavenly graces.

The object in writing these articles on precious stones is to introduce the readers of The Girl's Own Paper to their "habitats" or native homes, whether in mountain, rock, sea, or river, and to bring before them their characteristics and influence, and lastly to gather up their histories, which are often stranger than fiction.

The study is one of fascinating interest, and could we trace the individual career of some gems we should understand many an enigma in the history of nations, and gain a deeper insight into the mysteries of the human heart.

Not only have precious stones been favourites of wealth and fashion, but they have been studied with passionate devotion by men of science, and Mons. Babinet says that "the study of gems, which may seem frivolous when looked upon as mere ornaments, appears in another light when considered with regard to important questions of trade, and as connected with the two sciences of minerals and optics."

It would be of great interest if we were only to study under what conditions of soil, climate, and labour nature forms them; indeed, those who bestow upon precious stones the attention they deserve will be gradually led to acquire some knowledge of the geography, mineralogy, physics (natural objects) and chemistry of the countries which produce them.

It seems to us that everything that brings before us the treasures of Nature and the exercise of the genius of man upon them must be a healthy and interesting study, and one which lifts the mind above the petty cares of daily life.

In the study of precious stones, our thoughts go at once to the diamond as the king of them all, and as the most valuable; and yet this is not exactly correct, for the ruby has ten times the intrinsic worth of the diamond. But I do not purpose to commence with either of these, but rather choose the pearl as being specially the ornament of unmarried girls, for it is of all gems the most fitted to represent purity, grace of form, and exceeding worth.

CHAPTER I.

THE PEARL.

"As the rain from the sky
Which turns into pearl as it falls in the sea."—*Thomas Moore.*

"Ocean's gem the purest of nature's work."—*Dryden.*

Pearls are the only gems that derive nothing from art, and any attempt to improve them or increase their worth often turns out a complete failure.

Unlike other members of the aristocratic family of gems and precious stones, they are, as a rule, perfect in their native condition both s to form, colour, and purity. Their home or habitat is altogether peculiar to them, for while other gems are formed and brought up within the mine, pearls are born and bred beneath the water. Their origin is surrounded with mystery and has afforded matter for the imagination and poetic fancy in all ages of the world, for as we all know from experience, whenever a thing is incomprehensible it gives occasion to the wildest conjectures.

An idea very widely accepted was that pearls were the tears of angels captured by the oyster; while another equally popular was that they were formed of drops of rain falling into the open shell. This last is expressed in a quaint Oriental fable which runs thus : "A drop of water fell one day from a cloud into the sea ; ashamed and confounded on finding itself in such an immensity of water it exclaimed, 'What am I in comparison with this vast ocean ? My existence is less than nothing in this boundless abyss.' While it thus discoursed of itself, a pearl shell received it into its bosom, and fortune so favoured it that it became a magnificent and precious pearl worthy of adorning the diadem of kings."

An ancient writer expresses this same thought in the following words : "On the 16th day of the month Nizan, the oysters rise to receive the rain-drops, which are afterwards made into pearls." Again, "Columbus must have been astonished when he and his mariners, being in the Gulf of Paria, found oysters clinging to the branches of trees, their shells gaping open to receive the dew which was afterward to be transformed into pearls."

All these ideas are quaint and pretty, but alas ! not at all like the real facts.

We feel almost angry when we hear naturalists describe these most costly of products as mere deformities, and yet there is truth in the statement, for there is no doubt that pearls are formed by the oyster for the purpose of rendering harmless to itself the intrusion of any irritating substance, by coating it with successive layers of matter, like to that with which it lines its shell, or it may be an effort of the oyster to mend its shell from within after some injury done to it.

A very interesting example of this may be seen in the following incident related by Mr. Streeter.

"A shell was lately left at a jeweller's containing a fine pearl valued at £200. The owner thinking it would be more valuable if removed from the shell, gave the order for this to be done, and a piece of rotten oak was found at its base."

Two scientific French gentlemen being very curious as to the origin of the pearl, opened several of them and invariably found in the interior some foreign body like a small grain of sand, and were satisfied that this accounted for the formation, though not of course for its size, shape or beauty.

Linnæus believed that the pearl had its origin in a hurt received by the oyster, and it was this belief suggested to him the idea of creating the disease in the fresh-water mussel of Sweden, and thus manufacture pearls at will, but the attempt failed.

The Chinese, however, have been successful up to a certain point ; for instance, they insert tiny leaden images of their deities within the pearl-bearing oysters which gradually cover them with nacre.

But for whatever reason or purpose pearls are formed there is no doubt that they excel in value and surpass in beauty the choicest gem of rock or watercourse. They were valued by the Persians more highly than gold or any other article of adornment, and the Egyptians have always regarded them as the most precious gift of the ocean in which they have their origin, and worthy of the honour of decorating their deities.

Among the Romans they were regarded as symbols of beauty, purity and nobility, and as emblematic of marriage. There is a celebrated engraving on a sardonyx in Rome representing the marriage of Cupid and Psyche, who are joined together by a string of pearls, the ends of which are in the hand of the god Hymen.

The passion for pearls and other gems was carried to such an extravagant height in Rome that even Julius Cæsar thought it time to curb it. He issued an edict prohibiting the use of pearls to all persons who were not of a certain rank, and unmarried women were forbidden to wear precious stones or pearls. The consequence of this was that marriages increased considerably throughout the empire, for on no account would they be deprived of their ornaments.

Pierre de Rosnel, writing in the seventeenth century, shows how highly pearls were appreciated even then by the Romans. "The pearl," he says, "is a jewel so perfect, that its excellent beauty demands the love and esteem of the whole universe."

Among all Eastern nations they are supposed to be possessed of the power of preserving the virtue of their owners, and as an emblem of maiden purity, it is the custom still at weddings in India to present a pearl to the bride.

It is believed that pearls were among the earliest substances ever employed as ornaments, and as far back as we can look into antiquity they occupied the highest rank among them, but by what nation or individuals they were first worn cannot be definitely stated, though every circumstance points to India and the Hindoos. It is to the East we invariably turn for every rare and beautiful production of nature, whose office it is to charm the sense of man or gratify his vanity. An old historian says, "The beds of the rivers of India are of gold, and the waters flow calmly as though unwilling to disturb their rich sands ; the sea also casts up on its margin an abundance of pearls and precious stones, and herein consists the greatest wealth of the inhabitants."

In the Hindoo mythology gems play an important part. Vishnu is represented in the form of a handsome youth blazing with light ; in one of his four hands he has a shell, in another a lotus flower, in a third a club, and in the fourth a ring—a sudarsim—which, with the precious stone on his breast, sends forth a light that illumines the whole of the Divine abode.

The high honour in which precious stones and pearls have always been held is shown in the Bible, where we find them used to denote the highest degree of excellence and perfection. For example, the new Jerusalem was revealed to St. John under the figure of an edifice whose foundations were of precious stones, its walls of jasper, and each of its twelve doors formed by a single pearl.

The parable of the "Pearl of great price," and the phrase "casting pearls before swine," show that in our Saviour's time it was recognised as costly.

The pearl, with its unpretending and quiet lustre, its chaste loveliness and elegant simplicity of form has been a greater favourite with Easterns than even the diamond. "It has," says an old writer, "a fairness which so well befits and adorns the ladies who wear them that it would seem as though nature had made it on purpose for them." It has been said that there is only one object in nature more beautiful than a pearl, and that is a beautiful woman. The Talmud illustrates this by the following story: "On approaching Egypt, Abraham locked up Sarah in a box that none might behold her dangerous beauty. But when he was come to the place of paying custom, the collectors said, 'Pay us the custom,' and he said, 'I will pay the custom.' They said to him, 'Thou carriest clothes?'

and he said, 'I will pay for clothes.' Then they said to him, 'Thou carriest gold ?' and he said, 'I will pay for my gold.' On this they further said to him, 'Surely thou hast the finest silk ?' He replied, 'I will pay custom for the finest silk.' Then said they, 'Surely it must be pearls that thou takest with thee ?' and he only answered, 'I will pay for pearls.' Seeing that they could name nothing of value for which the patriarch was not willing to pay custom, they said, 'It cannot be but thou open the box and let us see what is within ?' So they opened the box and the whole land of Egypt was illumined by the lustre of Sarah's beauty far exceeding even that of pearls."

Beautiful and marvellous as these works of nature are, I think the most wonderful thing about them is the common material of which they are formed. Twenty-three parts of their composition are carbonate of lime and water, and one part of some gelatinous matter which serves to bind the whole together. As a rule these are the same materials of which the shell of the pearl oyster is formed, only that in the latter there is a little more vegetable matter. Although there is so great a resemblance between the pearl itself and the shell of the creature producing it, yet while the former is of surpassing value, the mother-of-pearl shell only fetches from £100 to £200 per ton.

So although we cannot fully and accurately answer the fool's question in King Lear, "Can'st tell how an oyster makes his shell ?" we are able to say of what it is made, and Mr. Streeter, who has had a pearling fleet for many years in the eastern seas, with scientific men on board, says that it is absolutely certain that the shell grows from within and not from the outside, and he gives the following as a proof. "There was found by our fleet in 1884 a shell that at a certain period of its growth had been broken, probably by a turtle, but the oyster had succeeded in secreting fresh layers of nacre within before harm came to it, and the old accident was only detected by the fracture at the back of the shell."

The oyster, although making use of the same materials for the forming of pearl and shell does not build them in the same way. In the first the layers, which are very thin, are concentric, that is having a common centre like an onion ; while mother-of-pearl has its layers more or less parallel, so that the latter can never have the same optical effects as the former. The outer layer of the pearl is friable ; the second is full of little cells in which the colouring-matter is deposited, and the inner ones are of a more foliated character. The peculiar lustre of the pearl is not derived from the substance of which it is formed, but by the varied reflection of light from the soft and gentle unevenness of its surface. I asked one of the greatest authorities on pearls what caused the variety of colour in the pearl, and I give you his answer. "The pearl, when taken from a healthy oyster, is everything one can wish ; if, however, the oyster goes out frequently to dinner and gets bilious, its pearl becomes yellow, and if it has fever its pearl is blackish." Many shells in sea and river produce pearls, but the finest called Orient pearls are found in a peculiar oyster, the best of which are known as the Meleagrina Margaritifera.

This high class pearl-bearing oyster differs greatly from the common oyster in that its two valves are equal, also that it has the power of spinning a kind of web which it can cast off and re-form at pleasure, enabling it to attach itself to bank, stone, or any other object ; it has also in a small way a power of locomotion, none of which characteristics are to be seen in the common kind. The Meleagrina, like all other oysters and mussels, produce a very large quantity of spawn, but so much is swallowed by its enemies that only a small portion succeeds in settling in its submarine habitat which is generally at a depth of from 36 to 48 feet. The pearl is generally found in the soft part of the oyster or attached loosely to the shell, and to be in really good condition the oyster should be at least three or four years old.

The pearl-bearing oyster is very much tormented by a little creature called the *honea*, which is very fond of feeding on it, and makes an entrance for itself by piercing the shell. The oyster resents this and rolls the pearl up out of the way of mischief, and uses against the intruder a little bag of acid which it carries in its beard, in the meantime making for itself a fortification with the over-flow of milk. And now it is time to enquire in what parts of the world we are to look for the habitats or homes of pearls, and by what process they are conveyed to ours.

In ancient times the principal fisheries or homes of pearls were in the Persian Gulf, the Indian Ocean, the Red Sea and Ceylon. These are still flourishing, but we have now additional ones in North-West Australia and America all well inhabited. As the methods of fishing are, in the main, the same, we will look into the pearl's home at Ceylon, because it was not only well known to the Phœnicians who traded here for pearls, but is even now one of the most prolific owing to the great care with which the fishery is conducted.

The special habitat of the pearl-bearing oyster is in the sand-banks off the west coast of the island in the Bay of Manaar about twenty miles long. These banks are favourites because they are sandy and interspersed with small patches of madrepore—a submarine substance like coral—to which the pearl-oyster attaches itself. They are arranged in seven lots which are worked in succession one every year. Should a portion of the bank be left longer than seven years it is thought that the pearls would so inconvenience the oysters that they would void them.

Early in the sixteenth century people of all classes collected here to the number of fifty or sixty thousand all intent on obtaining pearls, or at all events interested in the pearl harvest. In the seventeenth century the Dutch made this a very popular fishery by allowing the divers twenty alternate days to fish for themselves, and as many as two hundred thousand people assembled here at the fishing-time.

In the eighteenth century, owing to some quarrel between the Dutch and the Rajah, the beds were left untouched for thirty-six years, from 1760 to 1796, at which time the English gained Ceylon and reaped the benefit of the rest, which resulted in 1798 in a net profit of £140,000.

The fishing commences in February and continues until the middle of April, and great are the preparations made for it. The fleet consists of a hundred and fifty boats, each being from eight to fifteen tons burden, without decks, and with a stage on each side from which the divers descend.

The crew of each boat includes a master or head pilot, ten divers and ten other men who manage the boat and look after the divers, and last, not least, a shark-charmer, without whom the men will not stir. The distance between the shore and the banks is about twelve miles, and the time of departure is ten o'clock at night, the signal being the firing of a cannon.

The obtaining of pearls is a very difficult and dangerous operation, and those whose occupation it is submit themselves to long and severe training; they are restricted to a particular diet, and for some time previous to the fishing season their limbs are rubbed daily with oil.

When the day arrives for the fishing to commence, the divers meet on the shore and offer up their devotions, fee the shark charmers, and on reaching the banks strip themselves of

their dress, except a cloth round their loins, stop their ears with cotton wool, compress their nostrils by means of an instrument made of horn, and bind over their mouths a sponge soaked in oil which resists the water for a certain time. A net is fastened round their bodies, a heavy stone of reddish granite and of certain shape, weighing from twenty to twenty-five pounds, is hung on their feet for the purpose of hastening their descent, and in their right hand a knife. So furnished the divers throw themselves down the pearl bank, five at the time. As soon as they are down they cast off the stone from the feet, and with the knife loosen the oysters from the bank and collect them in the net; the average time of remaining under water is a minute or a minute and a half, in which eight or ten oysters are obtained. A signal is given and the men are at once drawn up, and while they gain breathing-time the other five divers go down. Native divers will descend forty or fifty times in the day, but the effect of this constant submersion and the strain on the nerves is seen in the faintness and bleeding from ears, nose and mouth of the men at the end of the season. The enemy most dreaded by them is the shark, and if alarmed at the near approach of one a diver signals to be drawn up to the surface, none of the others will go down on the same day. Few of the men engaged as pearl seekers live to old age, but while they can work they receive good and fixed wages. I hear that the majority of the divers in Ceylon are Roman Catholics and Hindoos. A peculiarity of the divers, and one that often stands them in good stead, is the dexterity and skill with which they use their feet; they can pick up the smallest thing from the ground with their toes just as easily as we can with our fingers.

On the return of the boats, they are unloaded and deposited in heaps as they are brought ashore, and left until they become putrid, when the pearls are easily removed from the tough matter surrounding them. The heaps are sold, as a rule, unopened, and their contents being unknown to both buyer and seller, the transaction is not so much one of commerce as a lottery. Many oysters contain no pearl, while others may produce one worth £200 or £300. Great care and vigilance are exercised during the washing which takes place for the separation of the pearls; but, notwithstanding, pilfering goes on more or less, the pilferers generally choosing the best pearls. These they often swallow for safety, but if suspected, the delinquent is placed in solitary confinement, and drenched with emetics.

Shells having pearls attached are handed to clippers, whose business it is to disengage the pearls by means of forceps. The part which adheres to the shell is polished by a powder made of pearls. In the year 1825 Captain Stewart related having seen ten pearls and some crushed oyster shells taken from the stomach of a fish called chartree.

The modern pearling fleet which fishes in the Indian seas, and off the western coast of Australia, uses the diving dress most successfully, and during its twenty years of existence the fleet has not lost a man to the sharks. The peculiar dress used by the divers has a little pocket at the side, easily reached by the man. When he notes the approach of a shark, he presses the bag, and out comes a certain acid, which, coming into contact with the salt water, illumines it, and frightens the shark, who is only too glad to escape.

The scientific men on board have made some interesting discoveries about the daily life of the oyster as lived in its submarine home. Some of these I am allowed to mention through the kindness of the owner of the fleet.

In order to keep a roof over its head it has to work incessantly to repair the mischief done

to its shell by the force of the currents swaying it to and fro, causing a constant wear and tear of its shelly home, which admits of no delay in mending.

When quite at its ease, and in good form, it opens its valves to survey its surroundings, and lays its beard wide open in perfect enjoyment; and wonderful to relate, it extends nearly a yard, and is of the most exquisite magenta colour.

Again, it is not generally known that each oyster keeps a general servant or scavenger, but so it is. In the Torres Straits the oysters employ lobsters to do their dirty work, while in Raeburn, Western Australia, they employ crabs.

There have been very good pearls found in our own rivers, especially in the Conway in North Wales, and in the rivers of Cumberland and Scotland; but the pearls of the Canadian rivers excel ours.

The number of famous pearls which have helped to make history is not large—seventeen or eighteen would include them all. Among these stand the "Cleopatra Pearls," one of which the Queen of Egypt dissolved in acid, and drank at a feast which she gave in honour of Antony. The second fell into the hands of the Roman Emperor, and was subsequently sawn asunder, and made into earings by Agrippa for the statue of Venus in the Pantheon.

Then about the same period, B.C. 44, there was the "Servilia Pearl," valued at £35,600 of our present money. It came to Julius Cæsar as part of the spoils of war in the East, and was given by him to Servilia, the mother of Brutus, A.D. 50.

The "Lolia-Paulina Pearls." This lady was the wife of Caligula, and possessed pearls and emeralds to the value of £400,000. These she inherited from her grandfather. "who," said Pliny, "became possessed of them by robbing and spoiling whole provinces." She appeared in public literally hung about with pearls.

Among those with a history is the "Sassanian Pearl," A.D. 500. It was considered a miracle of nature. The Sassanian monarch ruled Persia from A.D. 226 to 641, and the portraits of these kings always represent a huge pearl in the right ear. It seems that a daring diver obtained it by the sacrifice of his life from the custody of a shark. King Perozes lost it while fighting with the Huns. He was lured by the enemy into a pitfall, and, seeing his position, he tore the pearl from his ear and cast it before him. It was never found, although a large reward was offered for it.

The "Gresham Pearl." Sir Thomas had often refused £15,000 for it, but in order to prove to the Spanish Ambassador that his Queen and country were richer than the King of Spain and his subjects he foolishly ground this beautiful pearl to powder and drank it in a glass of wine to the health of Queen Elizabeth.

Another interesting pearl was "La Peregrina," A.D. 1579. It was pear-shaped, and pronounced to be beyond price. It came from the Panama fisheries, and the oyster from which it was taken was very nearly thrown away. The shell was so small that the fishermen considered it of no value, and were about to cast it back into the sea, when second thoughts prevailed, and on opening it, to everyone's surprise this magnificent pearl was discovered.

Another large pearl was brought from India and sold to Philip IV. of Spain for a sum equal to £18,000. It is pear-shaped, and believed to be in the possession at the present time of the Russian Princess Youssoupoff.

The "Shah Pearls." One of these was bought from an Arab at a cost of £56,000. Its shape was an almost perfect heart, which

uld detract from its value at the present
ie.

The "Hope Pearl," 1839. The late Mr.
nry Hope, of Piccadilly and Betchworth,
ik great pleasure in collecting pearls. The
gest was a baroque, a very fine specimen of
Oriental pearl of an irregular pear-shape
asuring two inches in length, four inches and
half in circumference, and weighing three
nces or 1800 grains. It was detached from
: shell, but it was deemed necessary to leave
mall portion of the shell adhering to it, but
ich is of so fine an orient and so well polished
it it is not distinctly perceived to be of the
ure of shell. This mass of pearl must
pass in the place the fish which formed it.
The "Russian Pearl" has a peculiar story
ached to it related by the traveller J. C.
hl, and which occurred about fifty years
i. He says, "There died in a convent,
ither he had retreated after the manner of
: wealthy pious ones of his nation, a rich
rchant. Feeling the approach of age he
l by degrees given up the toils of business
his sons. His wife was dead, and the only
oved object which even in the cloister was
; divided from him was one large beautiful
iental pearl. It had been purchased for
i at a high price, and so enchanted was he
its water, magnificent size and colour, its
fect shape and lustre, he would never part

with it however large a sum was offered for it.
He fairly worshipped the costly globule.
While he himself inhabited an ordinary cell in
the convent, this object of his love was bedded
on silk in a golden casket. It required very
powerful recommendations to obtain a sight
of it. No one ever dared touch this pearl of
pearls. During the last illness of the old man
he never let his pearl out of his hand, and
after death it was with difficulty removed from
his stiffened fingers. It found its way afterwards to the Imperial Treasury.

The "Southern Cross Pearl" is perhaps the
most remarkable production of its kind that
nature has ever produced, and it is by Mr.
Streeter's kindness I am able to give an
account of it. It consists of a group of nine
pearls; seven compose the shaft, one and a
half inch long, and the two arms of the cross
are formed by one pearl on each side. The
pearls are of fine orient, and would be of
good shape if they had not become slightly
flattened at the back. This cross of pearls
was discovered by a man named Clark while
pearl-fishing at Raeburn in Western Australia.
The owner of the boat was a Roman Catholic,
and both owner and finder were struck with
awe and amazement, looking upon it as a
heaven-wrought miracle, and with superstitious dread they buried it, for how long it
is not known. It was discovered in 1874,

since which date it has changed hands many
times, and was exhibited in the Western
Australian Court of the Indian Exhibition of
1886. It is valued at £10,000.

No one has been able satisfactorily to
explain the regular grouping of these pearls;
but it has been suggested by Dr. MacSarty
that a fragment of serrated seaweed may have
gained access to the shell, and that the
succession of teeth along the margin of the
frond may have determined the deposits of
nacre at regular intervals so as to form a
string of pearls running in a straight line. As
this cruciform group of pearls was found in the
Southern Hemisphere it has received the
name of the southern cross, from the famous
constellation so called.

The necklace of the Empress Eugénie contains a row of matchless black pearls.

There was in the market lately a round
black pearl of surpassing lustre weighing sixty-
seven grains;* the value of this has been
increased by finding another exactly like it.

It is computed that out of twenty million
oysters four million or one-fifth contain
pearls.

The medicinal qualities of pearls will be
shown later.

---

* Over twenty grains the pearl is equal to the
diamond in value.

NOTICES OF NEW MUSIC.

connection with two events of great in-
est—one especially to Europe and the Old
orld, the other to the New World of
nerica—we have received several musical
npositions. The enthusiasm and pleasure
h which the Royal Wedding was greeted
. brought forth much musical production,
od, bad, and indifferent, and there is
reely a music publisher in England who
. not produced his *Princess May Valse*,
Duke of York March, or *Royal Wed-
g Gavotte*. It is but a faint reflection
the national expression of joy and good
ling.

From the Chicago Exhibition we have re-
ed a very charming little collection of
ldren's songs, well got up, and published
Novello & Co. It is called *The Chil-
n's Souvenir Song-Book*. Anyone de-
ng to make their little friends a tasteful,
ful present should purchase a copy. Half
composers are American, and half are
glish, such well-known names as Mac-
izie, Stanford, Hubert Parry, Barnby,
ndegger, Farning, Tours, and Myles B.
ster, representing this side of the Atlantic;
ery interesting memento of the enormous
hibition at Chicago.

Songs.

My Heart is wi' My Lassie (R. Cocks)
a pretty Scotch ballad; the words by
bert Gilfillan, the music by Madge Conroy.
Is of Yore is a ballad of usual type, by
gelo Mascheroni.
I Question is the title of a very graceful
g, by George F. Horan, to words by
Emmens (J. Williams). This is likely to
very popular.

Part-Songs and Cantatas.

Popular Trios for Ladies' Voices (R.
Cocks), Nos. 38 to 43, contain six charming
compositions by Theo. Marzials, who is also
responsible for the words. Where all six are
so good it is difficult to make selection; but
especially pleasant are No. 38, *May-Day* and
No. 41, *Slumber Song*.
Love's Net (Forsyth) is an effective, if not
very powerful, madrigal, composed in four
parts by J. Clippingdale.
Robert's Mistake, a humorous trio for ladies'
voices, by J. W. Hartley. This is really a
humorous trio, and just the thing for Christmas
amusement.
Red Riding-Hood, an operetta for children, by Arthur Page. This little work for
quite young children may either be acted or
simply sung as a little cantata. For the
former arrangement, stage directions of a
simple nature are given. It is a pity that the
melodic interest is not more varied and graceful in design. Monotony for children is fatal.
A Christmas Dream (Novello), by Alfred
Moffat, and *Christmas Holidays*, by H. W.
Schartan, are new issues of Novello's School
Music, and form capital little cantatas for the
younger children, who will get much fun out
of the preparation and the acting. They are
printed in both notations.
Interval Exercises for Singing Classes, by
Florence A. Marshall, will be found so very
useful to teachers and sight-readers alike.
The design of the book is excellent and the
instructions are complete.
Florette, music by Agnes Bartlett (J.
Williams), is a rather ambitious but interesting
operetta for treble voices, founded on Grimm's
tale of the goose-girl St. Cecilia (Fifth Series).
Some very good new numbers appear in this

collection of two-part songs for treble voices;
amongst others, 8 two-part canons in unison,
by A. E. Horrocks; 12 two-part songs by
Joachim Raff; and *Give*, a two-part canon
by Myles Foster.
Unison School Songs include some of the
graceful and original melodies by Florian
Pascal to words by such excellent writers as
M. C. Gillington and Adelaide Procter. The
originality and beauty of Miss Horrocks's
music to Miss Gillington's words were never
more exquisitely shown than in two Fairy
Songs for treble voices. These dainty part-
songs will delight ladies' choirs where good
music is preferred to easy trash.

Piano.

A Complete Scale and Arpeggio Tutor, by
Adolphe Schloessen (Cocks), includes all the
requirements in this department for candi-
dates preparing for Trinity College, London,
and the Associated Board, the two repre-
sentative English Examinations.
Serenade, by Leo Stern, transcribed for
the piano by Benno Schönberger, is an
effective arrangement of the favourite piece
for violin and pianoforte.
Doushka (J. Williams), a polka-mazourka,
composed by Frances Allitsen, is a superior
teaching piece.
Of the same type is *Chopineski*, a homage
to Chopin's memory (Patey & Willis), by
Myles Foster, and a *Mazurka* (Williams),
in A minor, by Miss Horrocks.
An Album of Polish Dances (Williams),
by F. Morgen, is a most characteristic volume,
each composition, in a different way, being full
of local colour and interest.
Boat Song, by Miss Horrocks, is an excellent composition.

A LEISURE HOUR; or, THE GARDEN AT HOME.

SEE FRONTISPIECE.

THERE is a grey-walled garden, far away
From noise and smoke of cities, where the hours
Pass with soft wings among the happy flowers,
And lovely leisure blossoms every day.

There, tall and white, the spectral lily blows;
There grow the pansy, pink, and columbine;
Brave hollyhocks, and star-white jessamine,
And the red glory of the royal rose.

There greeny glow-worms gem the dusky lawn;
The lime-trees breathe their fragrance to the night;
Pink roses sleep, and dream that they are white,
Until they wake to colour with the dawn.

There, in the splendour of the sultry noon,
The sunshine sleeps upon the garden bed
Where the white poppy droops a drowsy head
And dreams of kisses from the white full moon.

And there, some days, all wild with wind and rain,
The tossed trees show the white side of their leaves,
While the great drops drip from the ivied eaves,
And birds are still—till the sun shines again.

And there, all days, my heart goes wandering,
Because there, first, my heart began to know
The glories of the summer and the snow,
The loveliness of harvest and of spring.

There may be fairer gardens; but I know
There is no other garden half so dear;
Because 'tis there, this many, many a year,
The sacred, sweet, white flowers of memory grow!

E. NESBIT.

AS CORNER-STONES.

THE similes that have been drawn from earth, air, fire, and water for the flattery or reproach of womankind would fill a volume. To throw together some of the more complimentary ones haphazard, we have been compared to stars, pearls, goddesses, June roses, violets, daisies, melodies sweetly played in tune, gazelles, jewels, birds, and sunshine! It seems indeed, for certain people, an absolute necessity to liken a woman to something, no matter whether appropriate or not, even as the bland Mr. Pecksniff called his daughter, who was not at all vocal, a "playful warbler." The master of all poetry suggests "a fountain troubled" as a fit emblem of an angry woman, and calls Cleopatra the "serpent of old Nile." Perhaps the most beautiful of ancient comparisons is found in the *Agamemnon*, of Æschylus, describing the arrival of Helen in Troy. It defies adequate translation, but has been thus rendered:—

"Even so to Ilion's towers there seemed to come
The spirit of a windless calm;
The gentle darling of a delicate wealth,
Soft dart of answering eyes,
Love's soul's-consuming flower."

In the Greek it is of course more musical, and gives an entrancing picture of "girlhood's subduing charm."

As a contrast with all that has been mentioned, the simile of a "stone" does not at first sight seem very attractive. The hardest, dullest, coldest of objects—what can there be in common between that and girlhood? How important it sounds! But in the Book of books there is even such a comparison, and it deserves close study. The whole verse runs thus—

"That our sons may be as plants grown up in their youth, that our daughters may be as corner-stones polished after the similitude of a palace."

Now it is a great mistake to pass by this familiar verse with a vague idea that it means nothing particular, or else that such expressions might have been all very well in Judæa centuries ago, but now have ceased to apply. The simile contains within itself just the teaching that is appropriate to modern ideas respecting womanhood, for the Psalmist in his aspiration after an ideal city catches the twin characteristics of perfect girlhood—Strength and Beauty.

Is it not so? That the corner-stone means strength, support, is an unnecessary suggestion to students of the Bible. Christ himself is called the "chief corner-stone" in several passages both of the Old and New Testament, and no one who has been in the habit of hearing sermons can have escaped many a full explanation of the appropriateness of that symbol. For the corner-stone was that upon which the whole structure depended. It bound together the sides of a building. Some of the corner-stones in the ancient work of the Temple foundations, Dr. Smith tells us, are seventeen or nineteen feet long, and seven and a half feet thick, while at Nineveh the corners are sometimes formed of one angular stone. It may be noted in passing that while the young men are to be "planted out," the daughters are to uphold and bind together the fabric

that shelters social life. One cannot press the comparison too far, but old-fashioned though it may seem, it must remain the work of the woman *par excellence* to make the home. If she does not do it, who will? All cannot; many must in these busy days be "planted out," yet the time-honoured task of home-making is not to be despised.

The conception of strength that can give support, as an ideal characteristic of girlhood, may be ancient, but still it is modern. The girls of the present generation are happily increasing in physical and mental strength. There was a pernicious idea afloat a quarter of a century or so ago, especially among young people, that it was "interesting" and suitable for a woman to be physically frail; to faint easily was an accomplishment much desired by the writer in her childhood, and by many girls of her acquaintance who could achieve nothing nearer the real thing than a "walking swoon," in which they were led poetically forth from hot or crowded places. Heroines in novels always swooned away on hearing any unpleasant news. The "genteel" education of girls in the backboard, stocks, and microscopic needlework stage at an earlier period still, was to blame for some of this mischievous nonsense. Now girls are encouraged to enjoy physical exercise—tennis, boating, skating, mountain-climbing, are familiar to them. The result of this changed order of things is a generation of taller, finer women than the last. The average girl now is decidedly taller than the average girl twenty-five years ago, and women who in their teens were considered to be of full average height,

ter Shaw, remember, paid the rent out of garden produce ; and if he could find a sel, why not we ? There will be plenty our own consumption to make our table itiful, I hope."

CHAPTER IV.

me now describe our retreat as it was n Camilla came to see us a month ago. honeysuckle over the porch was fully out, filling the air with its subtle fragrance. bad plenty of old-fashioned flowers under windows, that always stood wide open to it not only the sweet scents from our little *erre*, but also the delicious aroma of are's incense, that floated all about us from ds, and fields, and heathery common.

'e introduced our fashionable cousin to our us vegetable borders—not forgetting the ous onion-bed—and gave her quite a ied dissertation upon the capabilities of soil, its produce, and the labour and agement it required.

You see." said Lois wisely, "we feed it . We have found the ground and the ts require as much attention as a nursery of children. If you want them to grow be healthy, you must feed them properly, never stint. So it is with the garden, h seems always hungry ; so we fill it at : times, and it rewards us as you see."

imilla laughed heartily at the mixture of tables and flowers that grew in such profusion in close proximity. There were -flowers and lilies rearing their heads as hbours to the onions, rose-bushes rubbed nst cabbages, and the evening primrose d sentinel-wise side by side with the tall boke.

Anyone may see that this is a woman's en," exclaimed she ; "it is all so de-usly quaint and out of rule. I wonder : our head gardener would say if he it !"

I don't care in the least !" broke out Lois y. "We judge by results ; and if they ;ood, what more do you want ?"

imilla put up her long-handled eyeglass looked my sister comically up and n.

I think you are changed, Loïs," said she. ou used to be so pensive—not to say uid. Whence this energy, my dear ? r checks were lilies, now they are roses, your eyes are brighter and clearer than I remember them."

oïs laughed good-naturedly.

Then I am a living testimony to the intages of living in the country—of breath-pure, sweet air, of rising early, of having lays full of useful work and rare enjoy-t. Camilla, I am happy and contented."

You are aiming a few shots at poor me, I ose," said our cousin ; "but they have ed harmlessly by. I grant that your life seems one long tonic ; but what suits you ld not suit me. I should die of *ennui* ? amusements, no theatres, no concerts, no ds—"

he would have proceeded with the melan-y list of if I had not drawn her to our urite rustic seat, saying : " Let us sit here ile and listen, Camilla."

To what ?" asked she ; but I made a token ilence, and she leaned back submissively closed her eyes.

'e were protected from the north and east ls by the hill and woods that sloped away t and left of us. In front, below the road, fields of grass, and corn, and clover stretched away in varied tones of greens, and greys, and purple, over which the summer clouds swept shadows in endless succession. A gentle breeze fanned our faces, overhead carolled the larks, in the woods uprose the daily concert to which its feathered songsters treated us, unpaid and ungrudging, while every now and then the soft coo-cooing of the pigeons broke through the harmony without mar-ring it.

" This is very sweet and soothing," remarked Camilla, at length ; " in fact, the sounds and scents all around make me feel quite dreamy."

" Pastoral images and still retreats,
  Umbrageous walks and solitary seats,
  Sweet birds in concert with harmonious
    streams,
  Soft airs, nocturnal vigils, and gay dreams
  Are all enchantment,"

quoted I.

" Then, to be practical, in comparing the respective merits of town and country life, you reckon that what you gain by your life here, balances against what you have lost by leaving the great world ? " asked Camilla.

" No," replied I ; " the accounts do not balance. The charms and advantages of sylvan life and sylvan economy outweigh every other consideration."

" What—that of social intercourse as well, Bab ? Are you not cut off by the kind of existence you have chosen from the society of your equals ?"

" Of course we have not the same oppor-tunities for forming friendships, neither can we afford the time or spare the means for cultivating acquaintances promiscuously ; but we have friends—have we not, Loïs ? The country is not over-populated with gentle-folks hereabouts, and we only know, and care to know, those who think us worth the trouble of visiting. In that limited list we number the old rector and his wife, with whom we are always welcome, and who think it no con-descension to come and drink tea at Honey-suckle Cottage. There are one or two other nice people besides who do not turn up their noses at us, and there are a few who do ; but we can well afford to dispense with the-honour, shall I say ?—of their acquaintance. Our poverty makes us proud, I dare say, but I don't think it is a pride that does us harm, because it partakes largely of the nature of self-respect."

Camilla nodded as if she approved ; and Loïs here took up the thread I had dropped.

" We have no reason to complain of dulness," said she, " for we find plenty of human interests outside our little domain, though our friends' houses do not stand shoulder-to-shoulder, neither are there any elbowing crowds in the lanes. We have a share of parish work to attend to which we find quite to our taste, and now and then plenty of humble friends worth seeking out and culti-vating ; for, I assure you, Camilla, there is a great deal that is pleasant, entertaining, and instructive to be gathered from the sons and daughters of the soil, who have lived on it and by it all their lives, claim intimate acquain-tance with all its varied moods and tenses, and with whom the love of the country-side is almost a part of themselves."

" You cannot have much leisure," said Camilla, glancing over the flourishing garden, " what with your indoor and outdoor occu-pations."

" That is true enough," I answered. " We often go to bed as tired as any labourer ; but I have come to the conclusion that it is a misfortune to have very little to do. Health suffers for the lack of work—besides, it is demoralising. We find it so delightful after a long day's satisfactory labour—and labour which is for ourselves, too—quite a different thing to working for other people—to take our well-earned rest in the depths of a favourite chair, with a book that is greatly to our liking."

" Tell me now," said Camilla, rising to face us, and looking very earnest and thoughtful, " does it pay ? Are you quite satisfied with the results ? Have you no secret reservations, no longings for a different kind of life than this spent in your Arcadia ?"

" It does pay," we both replied. " We have had sufficient time in which to make the trial, and we have never once regretted it. We have been able to live more easily than we anticipated—quite within our modest income, and have, moreover, by dint of acting on the maxim ' Waste not, want not,' been able to put by—by driblets, if you choose—what has helped to render the long months of winter less trying to go through. And not that only ; but we have been so successful in the management of the garden that it has more than paid for itself. Why, we made £3 out of it last year, and we hope to do still better this year now that we understand better how to work it ! Tell me now, Camilla," added I, impressively, " do you honestly think that we could have done better if we had decided to remain in London ? What a miserable exis-tence it would have been ! How should we have dragged out the weary days, hardly knowing sometimes how to get a decent meal ? Why, half the money would have been swallowed up in rent ! "

" And I am sure," added Loïs, " you would infinitely prefer coming to see us here to having to trudge into some horrid cheap neighbourhood such as we should have been forced to find lodgings in ! A stuffy street, with houses all of the same pattern all let in apart-ments, a public-house at each street corner, no blue sky to be seen, no shady trees—can you fancy yourself, Bab, after this, shut up in such a hole, afraid to open the windows to air the hot rooms because of the dust that blows in, and for ever worried by the noises incidental to such a neighbourhood ? How we should pity ourselves ! "

" And behold us here," concluded I, stretch-ing out my hands to embrace the fair land-scape. " We are mistresses of all we survey. There are woods inviting us to explore their leafy glades ; there are hills that draw us nearer to the skies ; there are deep embowered lanes to attract ; there are birds and insects singing and humming all around, and all is ours to enjoy, while there is a dear little modest nest of a home just suited to our needs and our purses, where we can live free from em-barrassments and unfettered by conven-tionalities. Who, after tasting the sweets of existence in the home of nature, could sigh after the pleasures that pall in a crowded town, or could breathe in comfort its smoke-dried atmosphere."

" You have both grown too enthusiastic for me," said Cousin Camilla, stifling a yawn. " It is all very nice, and I congratulate you on your success and contentment. I think you are wonderful women, and I feel a most ordinary individual in comparison ; but, oh, Bab, if you don't mind, I am so thirsty, that the only thing I can go into heroics over just now is a cup of tea."

Whereat we laughed and repaired indoors on hospitable thoughts intent.

(To be concluded.)

MY LADY.

By M. HEDDERWICK BROWNE.

DOWN the broad oak-stair she trips
  With her floating filmy gown
Like a cascade shimmering down
  To her dainty, slim toe-tips.

With her gay and girlish grace,
  And her gleaming golden hair,
And her brow undimmed by care,
How she lights up the old place!

And I almost could declare
  That the high-born pictured dames
Look down from their gilded frames
  Wondering, "Were *we* e'er as fair?"

But I half resent the stare
  Of the *courtiers* on the wall
As she passes through the hall
  With the lamplight on her hair.

Oh! the wonder in her eyes,
  And the shy hopes in her heart,
As she goes to play her part
In the world that 'fore her lies.

And I kiss her on the brow,
  Breathing in my heart this prayer—
  "God go with you everywhere;
Keep you pure and good as now."

PRECIOUS STONES; THEIR HOMES, HISTORIES, AND INFLUENCE.

By EMMA BREWER.

CHAPTER II.

DIAMONDS.—*Hardness*, 10; *specific gravity*, 3'52–3'55.

"Those sparkling blossoms of the rock."

"What creatures here on earth have we
that are endued with so much sincerity, purity,
transparency, and splendour that are so fit to
resemble heavenly things by as these?"
—*Tho. Nicols, A.D.* 1652.

I HAVE already remarked
that the most wonderful thing about precious stones is the commonness and universality of the materials of which they are formed; and in no gem is this more noticeable than in the diamond, which is simply crystallised carbon, or carbon in a state of absolute purity.

It is a material found everywhere and in everything—in the bread we eat, in the coal and wood we burn, in plants and trees and flowers.

Uncrystallised it is brittle and opaque and worth but little; in its crystallised state, however, it takes to itself new qualities and becomes the hardest of all known substances, as well as the purest and most brilliant, and is often above price.

Another interesting circumstance is that the materials of which precious stones are made seem to have their doubles in inferior varieties, which are so like the true, that only the keen and critical observer can detect the difference, thus bringing to our minds the parable of the "Wheat and the tares."

For example, there is carbon and carbonate; the latter is of the same composition as the former, even possessing the same hardness; but it is black and lustreless, and will never have a chance of becoming a precious stone; but its existence is not useless seeing that its office is to enhance the value and brilliancy of its higher class sisters by cutting and polishing them. It seems to be the connecting link between uncrystallised carbon and the diamond.

Before a stone can be admitted into the magic circle of precious it must be proved to possess certain qualities born and bred in it.

Crystallisation is one of these characteristics, and when one thinks of the marvellous combination of circumstances required for the formation of these beautiful crystals, we know that only Mother Nature herself could be the author, only she, in her mysterious and patient method of working, could produce the exact amount and tint of colour, the necessary transparency, brilliancy, and lustre, together with the absolute freedom from defect and flaw which mark the precious stone.

Another quality inseparable from a precious stone is hardness; not as we understand it in common talk, but rather a power within it which prevents its being scratched or impressed by other stones. The diamond possesses this in the highest degree, and the two which come next are the ruby and the sapphire, which are simply crystallised clay. If a stone refuses to be scratched by these you may be quite sure it is a diamond. In a conflict between crystallised carbon and crystallised clay the former is always victorious because it is the hardest of all. Its hardness is represented by *x*, while that of the ruby and sapphire is stated at nine.

Hardness is the quality which allows the proper polish and lustre, and is, therefore, of great importance.

A circumstance which characterises the diamond is that neither solvents nor acids have the slightest power to dissolve or decompose it, while very great heat will entirely consume it, if applied in a special manner. A test of precious stones, well known to the ancients and practised in India many centuries ago, is what is called the "specific gravity" of a stone. It enables us to detect the class of stone without injuring it in the least.

To make it clear—two equal volumes of different substances very rarely have the same weight; a piece of lead, for instance, is heavier than a piece of wood equal in size. Bearing this in mind, it will be easy to understand that the specific gravity of a stone is the proportion its weight bears to an equal volume of water, and the way to arrive at this is first to weigh it in air and then in water, and to divide the weight in air by the difference between the weight in water. For example, suppose the weight in air to be 17 carats and the weight in water 12 carats, the difference between the two would be 5 carats. Divide the 17 by the 5 and you would have 3⅖ as the specific gravity.

Many qualities for which the diamond is valued, such as its lustre, transparency, refraction, and dispersion of light are only seen in a slight degree in the rough; in order to bring out these to the full extent they must be submitted to cleaving, grinding, and polishing.

An old writer, speaking of the diamond, says: "The true diamond is the hardest of all stones, without colour, like unto pure water, transparent. This property it hath that it will snatch colour and apply it and unite it to itself; and thus will it cast forth at a great distance its lively shining rays, for that no other jewel can sparkle as it will."

Before starting to see the diamonds in their homes it would be well to explain the carat by which precious stones and gold are weighed. Carat is the name of a bean, the fruit of a podbearing plant growing on the Gold Coast of Africa. When dried it is nearly always of the same weight, equal to four grains avoirdupois or 3'174 grains troy. In very remote times the carat was used in the chief market of Africa as a standard of weight, and it was subsequently introduced into India for weighing diamonds.

Diamonds are found in all parts of the world, but the best* and most valuable have their homes in the oldest mountains, which are composed chiefly of granite, porphyry, and mica slate; but even here they do not court attention. The rocks must be broken up into small fragments and the *débris* reduced to sand before the diamonds appear.

Many of the finest diamonds are, however, found far away from their original homes in alluvial soils; that is to say, in soil deposited by water, and in the gravels and sands of river-beds, having been swept away from their original moorings by heavy rains and rushing torrents; and in their passage from one bed to another they are often exposed to rough usage which would ruin them but for their natural attributes of hardness and density. Job seems to have been familiar with the habitats of precious stones, for we read, "He putteth forth His hand upon the rock; He overturneth the mountains by the roots; He cutteth out rivers among the rocks, and His eye seeth every precious thing. He hindeth the floods from overflowing, and the thing that is hid bringeth He forth to light."

The rocks, and the diamonds they contain, are of extreme antiquity, and probably had their place in the world long before the plants and animals had their existence in it.

* Oriental and Occidental originally were applied to precious stones in their literal sense, but at the present time they are retained, not to indicate the regions from which precious stones are brought, but rather to establish between stones of the same name a comparative value. The most precious variety of any precious stone is called Oriental, and the inferior variety Occidental, whatever may be the countries in which they are found.

"WITH THE LAMPLIGHT ON HER HAIR."

"They are," says a French scientist, "an inheritance to man from an age when there was no foreshadowing of his existence in the world."

The ancients valued and preserved precious stones thousands of years ago, investing them with an importance far above that they obtain in the present day. They attributed to them a spiritual and material power—a power to cure diseases, to avert calamity, and to drive away demons. "This alliance of religion with science is one of the distinguishing characteristics of antiquity," * and helps to explain many things. The vesture of the high priest, which was made "for glory and for beauty," was adorned with symbolic gems: he carried on his breast the emblems of purity, of glory, of light, of perfection, of truth, of justice.† The twelve stones were set in the form of a double square, the adamant, or diamond, being the third in the second row. During the Middle Ages the habitat of the diamond was quite as much a mystery as its composition, and many vague stories concerning it were formerly believed; one current was that when Alexander the Great approached the inaccessible valley of diamonds in India he directed pieces of meat to be thrown in, as the only means of procuring the gems. Vultures, it is said, picked them up with the precious stones attached, and dropped them in their flight.

The valley of diamonds was an article of belief to the Eastern world, and Marco Polo, who travelled in India in the thirteenth century, tells the same story of the manner of getting the diamonds, viz., by means of pieces of meat thrown into the crevices of the rocks. As to the composition of diamonds, there were many theories. One was, that precious stones were engendered by juices distilled from precious minerals in the cavities of rocks, the diamond being derived from gold;‡ another was that precious stones were living beings, one authority stating that "not only do precious stones live, but they suffer illness, old age, and death." The two opinions accepted at the present time are, first, that diamonds are formed from carbon by the action of heat; the second, that they are formed from the very gradual decomposition of vegetable matter with or without heat. The chemical composition of the diamond was not made clear, nor the history of its discovery completed till about forty-four years after Sir Isaac Newton's death.

The diamonds earliest known to the Romans were furnished by Ethiopia; but when Pliny wrote in the beginning of the Christian era they had already been brought from India, and thenceforth, until the eighteenth century, no diamond mines were known but those of the East Indies, in the empire of the Great Mogul, and of Borneo.

The first reliable accounts we obtained of the diamonds in India were from travelling merchant-jewellers, the most noted of whom was Tavernier. He was born in Paris in 1605, and spent forty years of his life travelling in the East, where he made a large fortune by trading in precious stones. He was the first to give a detailed account of the diamond mines, the manner in which they were worked, and the trade carried on in them.

Up to the beginning of the eighteenth century had the question been asked, "Where is the home of the diamond?" the answer would certainly have been "Asia;" and if for "the best home in Asia?" the reply

would surely have been "Golconda." But now, with increased knowledge and experience, we should acknowledge that the localities of the diamond are not confined to India, but include Sumatra, Borneo, Brazil, South Africa, parts of North America, and Australia. It is true that the first diamonds known to European trade were brought from Golconda. The discovery of these mines is attributed to a poor shepherd, who, while tending his flock, stumbled upon what appeared to be a pretty pebble. It must be remembered that there is nothing very attractive about the diamond in its rough state; there is neither brilliancy nor play of light to be seen. It has been thought that mines of precious stones emit light like stars; but this is not so, as the qualities of brilliancy and light are only brought out after man has removed the covering.

Well, the shepherd, knowing nothing of its value, exchanged it with a friend, as ignorant as himself, for a little rice. It subsequently fell into the hands of a merchant, who recognised its worth and eagerly sought for the home whence it had come. He found it and other mines as well, not in Golconda itself, but five or six days' journey from it, at the foot of the mountains near to the Kistna and Pomar rivers. When the diamonds were found in these mines, they were taken in the rough to Golconda, there to be cut, polished, and stored, and therefore called Golconda diamonds. The ground in which they were found was sandy, and full of rocks which contained many veins and fissures; the miners probed these with little iron rods crooked at the end, dislodging the sandy earth. Unfortunately, they were not always content with this, but gave the rocks such hard blows with levers of iron that they frequently produced flaws in the diamonds embedded within them. The next process was to well wash and carefully search the material, to see if it had any diamonds.

In 1669, there were as many as sixty thousand people at work in these special diamond mines. The number and size of the diamonds discovered were remarkable, but they were not, as a rule, of the finest water; to fulfil this condition "a diamond should be like a dew-drop hanging from a damask rose-leaf."

Tavernier asserted that the Great Mogul Diamond was found in one of these mines; if so, it was quite sufficient to distinguish these so-called Golconda mines, for few diamonds have had such a career. Indeed, the adventures and incidents belonging to it are startling. The time of its first appearance in the world (1630 to 1651) was one of trouble and conflict both in England and in India, and, like all other great diamonds, it seemed to bring ill-luck to its possessor.

Tavernier, who was the first European to see it, spoke of it as the heaviest of which he had any knowledge, and weighed in the rough 793⅗ carats. At the time he saw it it was in the Palace of Agra, which was for the time turned into the prison of the dethroned and stricken Mogul. "Brought to light in the midst of tumults and wars, the Great Mogul Diamond, after an existence of two hundred years, went out with the expiring flames of a great rebellion known in history as the Indian Mutiny." * It was probably stolen either at the sack of Delhi or at the death of Nadir Shah, and in order to avoid detection the thieves most likely had it broken by cleavage into two or more stones.

It will be a surprise to many that the chief negotiators in the sale of Golconda diamonds were boys under sixteen years of age. Tavernier gives a very pretty description of the

way they conducted their business :—" It is pleasant to see the children of merchants and other people of the country, between the age of ten and fifteen, coming every morning and seating themselves under a large tree in the market-place of the town. Each has his diamond-weights in a little pouch hanging on one side, and at the other a purse attached to his girdle. There they sit and wait until someone comes from the neighbourhood or from the mines to sell them diamonds. The new comer places the gem in the hands of the eldest of these so-called Golconda mines chief of the band. He looks at it, and hands it to the one next him, and so it passes from hand to hand in perfect silence till it returns to the first, who asks the price, in order, if possible, to make a bargain; and if the little man happens to buy it too dear, he has to take it on his own account. As soon as evening comes, the boys bring together all the stones they have bought during the day, examine them, and arrange them according to their beauty, their weight, and their clearness; then they put upon each its price at which they intend to sell to the merchants, and by the latter price they see how much profit they will have. They now carry them to the large merchants, and all the profit is divided among the boys, the one who acts as chief receiving one-fourth per cent. more than the others. Young as they are, they know the price of every stone."

It seems as though the diamond, from the first moment in which it is seen, sharpens the wits and arouses ambition for gain. Even the poor slaves in the days long gone by managed, as now, to elude the sleepless vigilance of the overseers. In one of these so-called Golconda mines Tavernier saw a poor creature, who desired to keep a large diamond for himself, force it in the corner of his eye so as completely to conceal it. That things are no better to-day, one has only to state what occurred a few months ago at the Cape. A known diamond thief was seen to leave Kimberley on horseback for the Transvaal; the police felt certain of the object of the man's journey, and seized him on the border and thoroughly searched him, and as nothing was found on him, they had to let him go. When well across the border and under the eyes of the detective, he shot and cut open his horse, extracting a large parcel of diamonds from its intestines, which, before starting on his journey, he had given to the horse in the shape of a ball.

Many of the mines round about Golconda, which were once so prolific, seem now to be quite exhausted. But in their place Brazil came to the front in a curious manner. In 1730, some singular pebbles were found by miners while searching for gold; these they carried home to their masters as curiosities. These in their turn regarded them as pretty baubles merely, and they either gave them to their children as playthings, or used them as counters.

At length they attracted the attention of an officer who had spent some years in India. Struck with their form and weight, he weighed one of them against a common pebble of equal size, and found that used as a counter much heavier; then he rubbed the counter on a stone with water, but could make no impression on it, while on the common pebble, which he treated in the same way, a flat surface was easily produced. He sent a few of the counters to a friend in Lisbon, begging him to have them examined; but the lapidaries of Lisbon, who had probably never seen rough diamonds, replied that their instruments could make no impression on them. The Dutch Consul, chancing to see them, thought they were diamonds, and begged him to send one or two of them to Holland; here they were cut and polished, and declared to be equal to the very finest Golconda diamonds. The astonishing

---

* Dieulafait.

† Mr. Streeter is forming a model of this breast-plate of real stones; it is most interesting and most beautiful.

‡ Pliny says, "The diamond is engendered in the finest gold . . . only a god could have communicated such a valuable secret to mankind."

* Streeter's *Great Diamonds of the World.*

Brazil, and all that were ounters or playthings were by a few individuals, and 1 in right good earnest.

ted like a curse upon the soon as the Government of these treasures, it took of the land, expelled the and declared itself sole

abundance to these poor ar of the discovery was and earthquake in which

numbers perished. "It seemed," says Emanuel, "as if the genii, guardians of the treasure, were indignant at the presumption of man, and tried by every means to prevent the dispersion of the buried treasure. As the news spread across the world the first effect was a panic in the diamond trade. No one would believe in the existence of a rival to the diamonds of India, but of course the Brazil diamonds could not be ignored. The two great mines were Minas-Geráes and Bahia. In the former 144,000 carats were found annually for the space of twenty years, and during

the first fifty years it is supposed that twelve millions of money's worth were exported. When once the search began, the riches were found to be almost without limit. The crops of all fowls killed were carefully examined, for it was found that in picking up their food they often swallowed diamonds, and it is recorded, that a negro once found a diamond of five carats adhering to the roots of a cabbage he had plucked for his dinner; they seemed to be about in all directions,

(To be continued.)

MERMAIDENS.

By SARAH TYTLER, Author of "A Young Oxford Maid," etc.

PTER VII.

TH HARBOUR WITH PRIZES.

eached England, Hya-ho was both quick and ilor, as bright as Tom, k-learning and natural nd cousin Perry—had conversational English nverse with us freely. long ago, but he had small services, and the had begun with fomen-ges promised to ripen ship. With the mer-s youth and his nation, ction that it belonged anhood to submit with the buffets of fortune, had grown reconciled ; which had sentenced ed *St. Barbe*—as dear i *Serpent* was to us—ners at the very com-career.

re ever such prisoners as the French showed atient and *débonnaire*, , ingenious, diligent, ng their greatest foes ioured *nonchalance!* e not known the best umstances are almost that they might never save prisoners and to afford the world an hearted courage and , but it was the men not the circumstances, which constituted the : *émigrés* who crossed a proportion of the anything rather than dignified resignation, iimple domestic virtue. and profligates, bring-he Royalist cause by excesses. They were 'rance men might live iy, a republic, or an iss through blood and ien brave soldiers, and ittle or nothing which g. It did not signify e the sons of princes, t of blue blood in their they were the scum of 'rgs, or were the most : *sans culottes* of the bscure departments. ar forward for his age ;

as an only son and an only child brought up on the paternal estate, he had been the little *gentilhomme*. Since his father had died in the boy's infancy, he had been the owner of the surrounding acres, the master of the servants of the château and of the peasantry on the soil from his earliest childhood. Widows' only sons are apt to 'be one of two things—effeminate molly-coddles tied to their mother's apron-strings, or precocious men with an exaggerated manliness. Sometimes the boys manage to combine both attributes, when the result is far from pleasing. It is that of a hectoring or a conceited *petit maître*, a young bully too early invested with authority, and at the same time a fop and epicure frightened to wet his shoes, or to have the wind blow on him. Hyacinthe did not illustrate this unhappy union of opposite qualities. He was strongly attached to his mother, but she had not made a girl of him in any respect. He was brave, with something of a man's quiet courage instead of with a boy's bluster. He was independent for his years without being self-assertive or defiant. His mother had not succeeded if she had ever tried in insinuating to him that he was superior to all other boys, a very model and paragon. He was secretly humble as well as manly in seeking to do his duty, and he gave all other boys, till the contrary was shown to be the case, the credit of seeking to do the same. He was too conscious of his lapses from his single-hearted standard to crow over his neighbours when they failed in their aim. He was the product of the Revolution, yet he had not entire sympathy with any side in the strife, which lent a certain isolation to his character and position, even in these early days.

There were other elements than those which were contained in the terrible overthrow of the nineties which had helped to build him up, mind and body. He came of a Huguenot stock in a Huguenot colony, to the immense, yet bewildered, relief of Aunt Maria, who counted all foreigners to be a blending of Romanists and infidels. Hyacinthe's ancestors' creed had caused them to stand somewhat aloof from Court and Court patronage of every kind, and had formed a special bond between them and the people on their estates, who were of the same religious persuasion, with a sen-

sible effect on the opinions and inclination of their descendant. He could not remember the horrors of the Revolution, but he liked to tell with pardonable pride how the Beaufois' peasantry had stood by their hereditary head and formed a guard round him and his, instead of putting a torch to his barns, plundering his *château*, and murdering the occupants.

Madame Beaufoi had continued something of a Royalist in politics. As to Hyacinthe, he was of young France ; but he was not devoted either to the Republic or to the Empire, though rather more to the first than to the last ; but he loved France passionately, and was willing to accept her choice of rulers. He was proud, as what French boy would not have been proud, of the unexampled triumphs and successes of her armies under Buonaparte and his marshals, and panted to serve her in any capacity. His youth led him to magnify a warlike service in whatever form. Captain Beaufoi, of the *St. Barbe*, was Hyacinthe's distant kinsman, and Hyacinthe drew from his mother her consent to his entering the French Navy as a midshipman on board the *St. Barbe*. Landward born though he was, he was fond of the sea in all her varying moods, and he promised to make a good sailor.

We passed Spithead with our "pickings" towed behind us, as the conquerors of the Old World returned in their ivory cars with their trains of captives. It was a beautiful day in July when we approached Portsmouth. Great crowds were assembled on the quays and at the wharves wild with enthusiasm. Multitudes of little boats swarmed out to meet and welcome us; the other ships manned their yards, cheered, and fired their guns as if we were royalty. Everybody afloat and ashore seemed to have taken leave of their senses.

I need not say that this public and triumphal entry was not father's desire, but he had to bow to the wishes of the authorities and the people when they sought to do the Service honour. I need not say again that we girls enjoyed the occasion, or that it was one of the proudest days in our lives, which we always looked back upon with gratitude and tender memories. We stood ranged in a row next Aunt Maria, a little behind and to the left of father and his knot of officers, in the centre of the quarter-deck, as the

THE TOMB OF QUEEN ELIZABETH.

e the Queen's, shading their faces. I heard afterwards elder was Princess Elizabeth, younger Princess Mary. The id to be the wife of the Landthe small principality of Hesseg. and grew to be so enortout that, it was said, if her burt circle had joined hands d not have encompassed her.* ager had a pathetic love-story.

to wait twenty years before cessities would permit her to r cousin—the sweetheart of her William Duke of Gloucester. not a man of great parts, and of the clubs were wont to call

Elizabeth was clever and painted well, distinguished artist Mary Moser, painted an entire room at Frogmore, with their

him " Silly Billy ;" but he kept his faith to his Princess like a perfect gentleman and true lover.

When their Majesties entered, we could not back any farther, but we made our best curtseys. The King said, " Eh, what ! my good Admiral Masham ? "—as if his Majesty had not expected to see father—" Come with your two hands full, as usual ! Not of French ships this time, but of the ladies of your family. Glad to present them myself to the Queen. Mrs. Masham and the Misses Masham, your Majesty. And you, my good friend Morehead " —addressing the master of the house—" and your wife and children. Glad to come and see you all, and to hear how my good city of London is flourishing."

As the King ran on in his loud, rapid way, nobody dared to interrupt him, or to correct his error in bestowing, with

out warrant, the brevet rank of father's wife and of the mother of his children on our maiden aunt Maria. We could only curtsey (afraid to look at Aunt Maria) to her Majesty, who bent her head with great dignity, just softened by a dash of affability, to us in return.

The introduction was not sufficiently formal for us to kiss hands ; however, the Queen condescended to engage Aunt Maria in conversation for a few minutes, and Aunt Maria told us afterwards that the Queen's remarks were exceedingly sensible and to the point, if a trifle dogmatic. Princess Elizabeth said a few words to Sally, and Princess Mary spoke in quite a sweet, friendly way to Jane and me. She asked if we were never sea-sick on board ship, and inquired if we had brothers sailors, mentioning that her favourite brother Prince William was a sailor.

"AUNT MARIA DRESSED HERSELF WITH UNUSUAL PAINS."

When the King was asking father questions which his Majesty answered himself, so that father could hardly find an opportunity to open his mouth, King George turned to us girls again and said, in his *brusque*, good-natured manner, "So I hear my gallant Admiral has provided himself with a family party of mermaidens, to bear him company in his cruises. Well, I can have no objection—none in the world—if they always bring us such good luck! 'Pon my soul, Masham, I believe it is to your mermaidens here that we owe your double success," he finished with a chuckle.

It was to this conversation that we were indebted for the term "mermaidens," which we first applied to ourselves in appreciation of a royal joke. Then our friends and neighbours picked up the word and attached it to us.

(*To be continued.*)

VARIETIES.

An Interesting Society.

Her father (interestedly) : "And you really enjoy your society for the higher culture of women?"

Minnie (enthusiastically) : "Indeed, I do, immensely."

Her father : "What was the subject yesterday?"

Minnie (reflectively) : "Oh, yesterday? Let me see. I think the question for debate was about some subject that some professor had been lecturing about somewhere, but up in a corner we talked about those new hats with the funny crowns."

Red in China.—A mystical meaning is attached by the Chinese to the colour red. No present is ever bestowed, even upon a white barbarian, which is not carefully wrapped up in red paper. The very name for present is *ang pao*—red parcel. Red is the colour of "longevity candles" and "birthday eggs." No Chinese gentleman would ever think of inflicting upon friend or acquaintance such an omen of death as a white visiting-card : it is always red. Red, in fact, is used generally on every joyful occasion, as at marriage, or at the birth of a male child, and is carefully avoided in cases of decease or mourning.

Inclined to Quarrel.—Should anyone wish to quarrel with you, remind her that it requires two to make a quarrel, and that you are not in it.

Seeking For Rest.

Anxious through seas and land to search for rest,
Is but laborious idleness at best :
In your own home the bliss you'll find,
If you preserve a firm and equal mind.

Bad Manners.—The manners of the ill-mannered are never so obvious, unbearable, and exasperating as they are to their own nearest kindred ; but this ought not to be. If we can be pleasant and courteous and well-mannered anywhere, surely it should be in our own homes, where the comfort of so many is dependent on us.

Repentance as It Should Be.—True repentance has a double aspect ; it looks upon things past with a weeping eye, and upon the future with a watchful eye.

Death a Necessity.—"I look upon death," says Dr. Franklin, "to be as necessary to our constitution as sleep. We shall rise refreshed in the morning."

A Test of Character.—A woman's character should be measured, not by her occasional exertions, but by the doings of her ordinary life.

Red-Letter Day.—In the olden time saints' days were regarded as lucky days, and were marked on the calendar with red ink. From this sprang the term "red-letter day."

Questions and Answers.

"Pray, how comes Love?"
"It comes unsought, unsent."
"Pray, how goes Love?"
"It was not Love that went."

An Alphabetical Curiosity. — The following sentence contains all the letters of the alphabet, and only five duplicates :— "Pack my box with five dozen liquor jugs." It will be noticed that not a single consonant is repeated in this sentence, the duplicated letters being all vowels.

The Right Sort of Girl.—A young man runs no hazardous chances in marrying a girl who is good, thoughtful, kind, and loyal to her mother.

Modesty and Pride.—True modesty and true pride are much the same thing. Both consist in setting a just value on ourselves—neither more nor less.

Simple and Great.—All simple people are not great, but all great people are simple.

Answer to Double Acrostic I. (p. 71).

1. L e o l F
2. O mphal E
3. V ictori A
4. E d g a R

Love.   Fear.

PRECIOUS STONES; THEIR HOMES, HISTORIES, AND INFLUENCE.

By EMMA BREWER.

CHAPTER III.

The rich diamond district of Bahia, which was the old capital of Brazil, was discovered in a very strange manner. At the time of the discovery it was a densely populated and fruitful province, and its agriculture proved its blessing and health. A slave from Minas Gerães, keeping his master's flocks in Bahia, thought he observed a similarity of soil to that of his native place. He sought therefore in the sand, and in a short time found seven hundred carats of diamonds. With these he fled and offered them for sale in a distant city. Such wealth in the hands of a slave raised suspicion and he was arrested, but would not betray the secret of how they had come into his possession. At length he was given over to his master, who also failed in obtaining the confidence of the man, and therefore resorted to cunning : he restored the slave to his former occupation in Bahia, without penalty or punishment, and had him strictly watched, and readily found the solution.

As soon as the secret became known, numbers of people came flocking in from Minas Gerães and other parts of Brazil, so that the following year as many as 25,000 people were occupied there in searching for diamonds.

In 1846 and 1847 Brazil was obliged to pay her debt in diamonds, which caused a depreciation of this precious stone, reducing it from £10 to £4 or £5 a carat. The rich field of Bahia diamonds was about eighty miles long and forty miles broad. Efforts were made to ensure honesty among the slave-miners by rewards for it. If a slave found a diamond of 18 carats, he was crowned with flowers and led in a triumphal procession amid the rejoicings of his friends to the manager, from whom he received his freedom, a suit of clothes, and permission to work for wages ; but, notwithstanding, one-third of the produce is supposed to be secretly disposed of by the workers. In the very presence of the overseers they manage to conceal them in their hair, their mouths, their ears, and between their fingers. One of the celebrated diamonds of the world, the "Star of the South," was found by a negress engaged in the works at Minas Gerães in 1853 ; it weighed before it was cut 254 carats. She received her freedom and a pension for life in recognition of her exceptional find. The owner sold it for £3,000, so little did he know of its real value. Its fame reached the remotest corners of the globe. It was forwarded to India, and a bid made first of £110,000. This fell through, and eventually it was purchased 1881 for £80,000, exclusive of the mountings, which were very costly, by the ex-Gaikwar of Baroda. "But," says Streeter, in his *Great Diamonds of the World*, "the ill-luck which seems to follow the possessors of great diamonds, overtook the new owner of the 'Star of the South.' He fell into trouble for the murderous practice of destroying his refractory subjects with diamond-dust, and, having tried the same to get rid of the British resident in Baroda, Colonel Phayre, whose presence acted as an inconvenient check, the Gaikwar was arraigned and found guilty, and deposed henceforth from the throne of his ancestors."

The discovery of the Brazil diamond-districts created, as we have seen, an excitement in the world ; but the opening up of the diamond-fields in South Africa, considerably more than a century later, created a panic and excitement no less striking.

The discovery of these vast riches was brought about in as simple and unpremeditated a manner as in the case of Golconda and Brazil.

Somewhat more than a quarter of a century ago a child of Jacobs, a Dutch farmer, settled at the Cape, amused himself by collecting pebbles from the neighbourhood of the farm, which was near to Hope Town. One of the stones he picked up was sufficiently bright to attract his mother's notice, and she put it on one side; but in the midst of household cares it was forgotten, until a neighbouring farmer came to see them, who was curious in the matter of stones. He was puzzled with its appearance, and offered to buy it of Mrs. Jacobs; but she laughed at the idea of selling a common pebble, and willingly gave it to him. Subsequently it was submitted to Dr. Atherstone of Graham's Town, who was an excellent mineralogist; but even he had some difficulty in deciding what it could be. After careful examination, however, he pronounced it to be a genuine diamond. It was sent to the Paris Exhibition as the greatest novelty the Colony could exhibit. Here it remained during the whole of the summer, examined by learned men of all nations; and, at the close of the exhibition, Sir Philip Wodehouse, the Governor of the Colony, purchased it for £500, and it was sold by him to Garrards, who cut it as a brilliant. Its weight was 21½ carats.

This is the simple history of the first Cape diamond.

In the autumn of 1868 news reached us from Cape Town that diamonds had been found on the gold districts on the Orange River, midway between the east and west coasts of South Africa, and if any doubts existed as to the truth of the statement, they were utterly put to flight by the discovery in the following spring of the African Koh-i-nor or Star of South Africa, valued at about £30,000. It was purchased by the late firm of Hunt and Roskell, by whom it was cut and sold to Lord Dudley. It is now known as the Dudley Diamond. It is of a light yellow colour beautifully crystallised, and in the rough the size of a small walnut. This stone was found by a poor herdsman who disposed of it for five hundred sheep, ten head of cattle and a horse, and was made very happy by the exchange. The origin of the Kimberley and Du Toits pans was, that a Dutch Boer named Van Wyk, who occupied a farm-house in this locality, was surprised to find diamonds actually embedded in the walls of his house, which had been built of mud from a neighbouring pond. This led to an examination of the surrounding soil, and the diggings thus commenced formed the celebrated Du Toits pan. The habitat of the diamond is not the same in Africa as in other diamond localities. Instead of being in the rock itself, the home is beneath it in a soft soapy mineral soil known by the name of blue earth, which in some parts has a depth of 450 feet and is reached by shafts. While I write I have before me, by favour of Mr. Streeter, one of the very few African diamonds embedded in a rock, and beside it a ruby, the rock being about the size of half a walnut. I have also before me a diamond about the size of a large pea, which from continual washings of thousands of years, has become perfectly round; this is rare indeed.

By 1870 public attention had become thoroughly roused; every town of South Africa emptied itself of men for the diggings, and diamond hunters poured in from every quarter of the world.

The South African diamonds are found over many square miles of territory. The area reaches as far as Pretoria, the capital of the Transvaal, on the north, and south of the Orange River to the north-west of Hope Town.

Jagersfontein and Mamusa are well-known localities for diamonds.

The diamonds are found also in the beds of rivers and what are called pans or dry diggings, such as Du Toits pan and Kimberley. A pan is a local depression in the flat basin-like hollows which extend often to a length of two or three miles. They receive the drainage of the surrounding districts, but having no outlet, the water, as it evaporates, acquires a brackish taste, and in dry seasons the pans exhibit a whitish saline incrustation.

It is supposed that in 1871 the diamonds ex-

DIAMOND-POLISHING.

ported from the Cape were of the value of £1,500,000, and there have been more large diamonds found here in a short time than in centuries in other parts of the world. Up to the spring of this year, 1893, the three great diamonds of the Cape were the Dudley, the Stewart, and Du Toit I.; but in June last the largest ever known was found in the New Jagersfonstein Company's mine in the Orange Free State, and is known as the Excelsior. Its weight is 970 carats and its colour is blue-white and almost perfect. It has some black spots in it which it is said can be cut out; it is supposed by some to be worth half a million. It was found by a Kaffir working in the mine shortly after blasting, in company of a red diamond; he received for his find £150, a horse, saddle, and bridle. The extraordinary thing about it is that some gentlemen were under contract to buy all stones good, bad, and indifferent at so much a carat within a certain time from this mine. The contract terminated on June 30th, and the Excelsior was about the last stone found on that day. It is about 3 inches high and 2 wide, while the flat base measures nearly 2 inches by 1½. It is now I believe in London.

Mr. Streeter, who has had great experience in the South African mines, tells us that "20 per cent. of the Cape diamonds are of the purest water; 15 per cent. of second quality, and 20 per cent. of third quality; the remainder, being too impure for cutting, is known as bort, which when crushed is used for grinding diamonds and engraving gems." Strange to say, that the black impure variety of the diamond known as carbonado, so common in Brazil, has not yet been discovered here.

I read in the *Times* on September 14th just passed, "Cape Town, September 13th."

"The De Beers Company have sold the whole of their remaining stock of diamonds for cash to Messrs. Barnato Brothers, who lately bought £1,000,000 worth of diamonds."

The De Beers Company represent the interests of the De Beers, the Kimberley, the Bultfontein, the Du Toits pan and other smaller mines which are close together and all discovered within a space of half a year, an amalgamation brought about by Messrs. Rothschild and Mr. Cecil Rhodes.

It was formed in 1888. It has a capital of £8,000,000, and in two years gave out some 2,500,000 carats of diamonds, realising by sale more than £3,500,000 produced by washing some 2,000,700 loads of blue earth, each load representing three quarters of a ton.

In working the mines, 1300 Europeans and 5700 natives are employed.

Lord Randolph Churchill, who has lately been to the Cape, says that the De Beers and the Kimberley mines are probably the two biggest holes which greedy man has ever dug into the earth; the area of the former at the surface being thirteen acres with a depth of 450 feet, while the latter is larger and deeper, the daily produce of the consolidated mines being about 5500 carats. There is one thing about the Cape diamonds which would to my mind make them preferable to those of India, they are free of the terrible histories which cling to these last.

"Could the many jewels that have found their way to England since the Indian Mutiny bear witness to the circumstances under which they have passed from the possession of their Indian owners, we question," says one, "if the European fair one could dare to deck her brow with those dearly-bought gems."

The letter of the *Times* correspondent with the army at Lucknow had the following passage in it. "Ere this letter reaches England, many a diamond, emerald, and delicate pearl will have told its tale in quite a pleasant way of the storm and sack of the Kaiserbagh. It is just as well that the fair wearer—though jewelry after all has a deadening effect on the sensitiveness of the female conscience—saw not how the glittering bauble was worn or the scene in which the treasure was trove."

It seems as though the diamond needed even in history a background to show up its dazzling brightness.

Australian diamonds have not yet made any great excitement, for the reason that they are so difficult to cut; they hang on the wheel, and the lapidary who works by the carat prefers those which are most quickly manipulated. A great authority told me two days ago, that if the time should come when the lapidary can work them easily, they will make a great stir in the world, for there are plenty of them and of good quality.

(*To be continued.*)

MUSIC.

I. E.—Should you pass your examination successfully you would be fully qualified to teach children, provided your method of conveying instruction were both agreeable and suitable for their easy comprehension. You will need patience. The science of harmony can be learnt without a master by some up to a certain length; counterpoint should follow afterwards.

GERTRUDE DEAR. Go to a music-publishers, and ask the favour of trying a few pieces suitable for the American organ, and select those within your own musical powers to play. They will show you both instruments and the differences between them. Why does anyone—besides "Medicus"—prefer to use a *nom-de-plume* rather than their own names?

ENQUIRING MIND.—Like your music-master, we have never heard the term before, and believe, therefore, that its use is quite non-essential.

M. M.—A book of instructions suitable for beginners in learning to play the piano can be procured at any good music-shop. We cannot name any special book, as we have often told our correspondents.

MISCELLANEOUS.

NUT-BROWN.—1. We cannot give you a prescription for making you fair.—2. Wearing gloves may improve the appearance of your hands.

DORIS.—Do your duty to your grandmother, who now supports you, and pray to God to take you into His care, and direct you should you survive her.

MIGNONETTE.—1. "It takes two to make a quarrel," so if you do not choose to be one contending party, there can be no quarrel. Again, remember the words of Holy Scripture, "A soft answer turneth away wrath," and if you must give an answer, do so in the spirit of this admonition, retraining your anger for Christ's sake.—2. Should your deafness proceed from a cold, a doctor might prescribe a tonic for it. Perhaps there is a hard accumulation of wax which he might remove by syringing.

JOAN.—One of the best and most easily procured insecticides is the water in which potatoes have been boiled, especially if the potatoes have been cut open. Wash your little fancy terrier with it. We believe it will destroy the parasites in which mange originates, owing, it is said, to the solanine, which is one of the constituent parts of that vegetable. It might also destroy the vermin which infest the leaves of plants.

NEWSPAPER.—You ask us to give you a remedy for a complaint for which no properly diplomaed doctor has yet discovered any panacea. Some sufferers from neuralgia find relief from one course of treatment, some from another. Much has to do with the locality in which the sufferer lives, the nature of the diet, the amount of mental and physical labour, the rest they can enjoy, the hereditary characteristics of the general constitution. As you are personally unknown to us, we could not prescribe for you, even were we medical practitioners; but we agree with you that whiskey and brandy are not desirable as palliatives. Good food, rest, change of air, and a residence on a gravel or sandy soil may do much for you.

NICHE.—October 5th, 1860, was a Friday.

MARY K.—The measurements you send are very large; but the largest cut stones in the world are said to be those in the Temple of the Sun at Baalbec, some of which are 60 feet long, 20 feet wide, and their depth cannot be ascertained.

MANCHESTER.—According to scientists, thunder has nothing to do with making milk sour. The atmospheric conditions which prevail during and just after thunderstorms, are only concerned so far as they furnish a favourable time for the fungus to develop rapidly. This fungus-growth is what really does sour the milk, and it is peculiarly fatal to young children who are at the nursing age.

CLARA.—1. We thank you for so kindly expressing your approbation of our paper, and especially our dress articles and their illustrations.—2. Your handwriting would be good if you shortened the tops and tails.

LOTTIE and E. W. F.—We cannot advertise shops. You must show specimens of what you can do where such things are sold, and obtain trade orders.

ANGLO-INDIAN.—You may bow slightly in passing to men with whom you have played at lawn tennis.

SORROWFUL.—In these days the period of mourning for a widow is two years. Crape is worn for one year and nine months, after which black only is used. The dress for the first year is fully covered with crape, and for nine months of the second year the dress is trimmed with crape. But some widows wear black only after the first year. The lawn collar and cuffs are usually worn only with crape; the veil and cap are worn for a year. The cap for the house is optional. The ornaments should be of jet with crape. A widow, however, in the present day, is really "a law unto herself." It depends on her own feeling. Many widows never leave off mourning, and use the bonnet and cap always with black.

"THE EARLY BIRD."—A new "Early Rising Club" has been started by Miss Emily Hartland, the Secretary of a popular "Practising Club." Address, Newent, Gloucester, and enclose a stamped and directed envelope for the rules.

"FIVE LITTLE SISTERS."—The quotation to which you refer is from a poem of the poet Gray—

"Where ignorance is bliss,
'Tis folly to be wise."

See "On a Distant Prospect of Eton College," stanza 1.

HARDY PLANT.—We are surprised that, as a professedly Christian girl, you have no shame in making such a statement, and asking such a question! Were you a Jewess we could understand your seeing no obstacle in the relationship; but as a Christian, you should need no one to tell you that you are, in heart, guilty of breaking the ninth commandment, and yet you have the shameless impudence to inquire "whether there be any harm in it?" From henceforth keep carefully out of his way, and should there be any difficulty in so doing, make a confidant of your mother, and ask her to aid you in so doing. Also humble yourself before God, and pray for both help and pardon.

HOPING FOR BETTER TIMES.—We never recommend Mr. Anybody's cure for either stoutness or thinness. We are not quacks, nor should we, as editors, be expected to be medical practitioners. Leave the little extra layer of fat alone, for, if well, any change will be to make you ill.

A. B. and F. R.—St. Elizabeth was the daughter of the King of Hungary. She was born in 1207 A.D., and betrothed in early childhood to the son of the Landgrave of Thuringia. She was devoted to works of charity, was under the severe rule of a priest, and cruelly treated by her mother-in-law and the family of her husband, who was himself much attached to her, but too feeble in character to protect her. One day she was asked by him to show what she had in her mantle, which happened to be supplies for the poor of Eisenach, and on insisting to see, the legend says the food was changed into white and red roses. To her bitter grief her husband joined the crusade in 1226, and died on his way at Otranto of fever. His brother then seized his possessions, and turned the widow out of the castle in the midst of winter. She kept herself from starvation by spinning till the knights returned, who dethroned the cruel usurper, made her son, Herman, landgrave in his father's place, and bestowed the city of Marbourg on Elizabeth, who lived there with her daughters. We have not space to tell you more than that she died early of severe austerities insisted upon by her priest, and deeply regretted.

AMY.—Yes; there are red or pink sapphires. One from the mines of Ceylon was sent over here, weighing 211 carats, of a pink colour. It is not the hue, but the composition of the gem that determines its character. Of all the fine red sapphires that have been known, and proved as being such, but few have weighed more than five carats. The largest known—for they are usually small and defective likewise—is to be seen in the Toison d'or of the French regalia. There are also yellow sapphires.

MARIE.—To cleanse the rose-tree from the green-fly blight, wash well with strong potato-water or tobacco juice.

HEART-BROKEN ONE.—If your "intended" have expressed a desire to be free on leaving England, let him have his liberty, and do not imagine that the breaking-off of the engagement is only for your sake, and a purely unselfish sacrifice of his own wishes.

HELEN. The French phrase, *Telle est la vie* means, "Such is life." There is no "d" in the word "oblige," nor an "e" in "truly." We draw attention to these mistakes, because they are so frequently made by our correspondents.

NONESUCH inquires, "Is it possible for a young man to love you thoroughly" (we correct both spelling and grammar) "who lives in the same house of business?" We are at a loss to comprehend what "living in the same house has to do with 'love?'" If any influence be the result of propinquity, it would be that more intimate acquaintance and opportunities for observing the habits and character of another, it would be to warm a friendship into a lover's attachment.—2. We have no recipe such as you require.

A. T. HALL.—We can only give you the often-repeated answer: apply at the various offices of the Mail Steamships Companies.

DOCTOR'S DAUGHTER.—1. It is better to be satisfied with one cup of tea at a friend's house in the afternoon, for if everyone asked for two, it would necessitate the making of fresh tea.—2. The eating of sweetmeats tends to create acidity in the system, which produces cramp, rheumatism, gout, and many other complaints, and injures the teeth. Once in a way two or three would do no harm.

OYSTERS.—The lines—

"Call us not weeds—
We are flowers of the sea."

are to be found in the poems of Eliza Cook.

CARRIE JOHNSTONE.—See "G. O. P.," volume xiii., pages 20, 220, 332, 362.

MEELVAH.—Read St. John, xxi, 21. We only know what is commanded, and therefore what is our own unquestionable duty. "He that keepeth My commandments, he it is that loveth Me." Certainly, as a believer, and one who desires to serve her divine Lord and Master, you should be forthwith baptised. But whether after the rites of the Church of England, or of any dissenting community, we can only leave to your own decision after much careful thought and prayer.

LONELY LASSIE.—We feel for your most trying position; but you are in the path of duty in remaining with your mother. Endeavour to draw the nearer, in your isolation from those you love, to "Him that sticketh closer than a brother."

S. S. M.—We can only advise you to write direct to the Matron or Lady Superintendent of the institution at Zeals, near Bath, and send a stamped and directed envelope for the prospectus and any written information they might be so good as to send you. It is best to obtain it first-hand, and a list of vacancies, if any.

A MOTHER.—We strongly recommend the "Ministering Children's League" to the attention of all who have young people under their charge and training. It was founded by the Countess of Meath in 1885. There are 240 or more branches now, spread from our own land over the colonies, the West Indies, and the United States, 18,000 and upwards of children being united together under the rule of the League—to "try to do at least one kind deed every day." At Ottawa, under their local president, Lady Lansdowne, they have instituted a convalescent home, and have made quilts, pillows, and other necessaries for the cots, and the little West Indian boys have turned neglected and disused graveyards into gardens. Great results have followed the efforts and practical work of infant hands, and those who are conversant with that universal characteristic of children—the love of doing something not within the limits of mere play, and their zeal in all they undertake (lessons generally excepted), will recognise the expediency of turning their thoughts and directing their efforts into so good a path. The Rev. C. J. Ridgeway, Lancaster Gate, W., started the first branch of the League in his parish.

INVALID.—Write to Messrs. Maclure, Macdonald & Co., Glasgow, for the address of the "Shut in Society."

IVY.—We sympathise with you in your loss of a friend. But you should learn the rules of metrical composition before you attempt to write verses. Even the rhymes are not correct—"love" and "good" do not rhyme; and the grammar and spelling need correction.

She explains to me that it is for the Procession that is to take place in the castle grounds to-morrow to pray for rain, the excessive drought having done irreparable damage to the crops.

After this I sit down to dinner and beg Blanche to keep me company, for I have a lively horror of "sweet solitude," especially at meal times.

I find the soup sour (although it has been made fresh on purpose for me), and (as the heroines in novels are said to do) I trifle with my chicken-and potatoes.

Blanche eyes me anxiously, for she knows that my appetite as a rule "faileth not," and as I push away my pudding untouched she says "That's had."

"It is," I answer shortly, and forthwith undress myself to go to bed, trusting that a dose of "Nature's Sweet Restorer" will alleviate my sufferings, freshen up my wits and restore to me my normally good appetite and temper. Unfortunately my sleep has not had the effect anticipated, as I have had a most ridiculous and uncomfortable dream, in which, I imagined that like King Théseus I was condemned to sit still on a chair for the rest of my life. My chair was a cane-bottomed one and very hard, my hands and feet were tied together, and a fly (of somewhat the same dimensions as the one I had encountered the previous morning) had began to march up and down the bridge of my nose. In vain did I turn, and twist, and shake, and wriggle, still did that animal walk gently backwards and forwards. In vain did I squint at it and make horrible grimaces; there it remained, and, unconscious of my agony and contortions, continued its nasal promenade. Suddenly, with an effort,

I freed my right hand from its cords, and woke up in the act of vigorously scratching my most prominent feature, as a consequence of which it assumed a sanguinary hue.

Tuesday, June 20th.—The moment my consciousness awakes my queer little bell clock tolls the hour of five, and I run to the window to have a look at nature at that cold, unsympathetic hour. A slight mist is over the land, and every rose, lily and carnation looks as though it had been dipped in crystal. The gooseberries, pears, and apples which are just beginning to ripen hang loosely on their stems, as though awaiting the sun's bright beams to warm them into life and energy. The spreading branches of the trees are so laden with dewdrops that every now and then as they sway backwards and forwards they water the earth with a miniature shower-bath.

As a rule I don't like rising before the sun has warmed the earth. When I awake I like to be greeted by the bright rays of the god of day, to hear the birds singing in the trees, and to see the flowers and fruit-trees glistening with light, and the sea rippling and reflecting its brilliance.

I fear these sentiments are not very praiseworthy, as the Bible, speaking of a perfect woman, says that "she rises before the day," and Monseigneur Dupanloup, the famous Bishop of Orleans, who is immensely read and quoted in this part of the world, affirms that "she who leaves her bed at five every morning has already traversed a great part of the road to Salvation." Preparations are going on in the little chapel for the procession, and I can see by the queer, faint light proceeding from the stained glass windows that the tapers are being lit. A rudely carved, but very ancient

statue of the Virgin, with the crown of its head, tip of its nose, two hands, and one foot missing, has been brought to light and placed in a conspicuous position near the porch. All this I can see, the interior of the chapel I have to imagine.

St. Cado and St. Anne, according to Blanche, have been well cleaned and dusted, but whether this process has improved their appearance, or made their chipped noses and toes less evident, I am unable to say. Blanche also tells me that four huge bouquets of roses and syringa have been placed on the altar, no doubt to hide as far as possible the ancient picture behind. O that picture! Words fail me when I try to convey a slight idea of its hideousness. St. Michael in bright red with a sword of gamboge, and wings of violet, is standing on a Satan in blue. In the background is the castle shockingly out of proportion, and in front are two ancient representatives of the house in which I am staying, who are certainly a pair of the wickedest-looking creatures imaginable. Though painted in the attitude of prayer, they are regarding each other with a malignant smirk, and I affirm (having often tried the process myself) that if one looks steadily at them for about five minutes, their already distended mouths seem to open wider and wider, until they reach from ear to ear, and the malignant smirk turns to a diabolical grin!

But enough of this picture. I leave my imagination and the chapel to take a view of the stone-barrier of the castle, of which I can get a glimpse by craning my head out of the left-hand corner of the window.

(To be continued.)

VARIETIES.

A CHOICE OF HOTELS.

Stranger: "Which is the better hotel to stay at here?"

Resident: "Why, sir, it doesn't matter which av thim yiz takes, for afore mornin' ye'll be wishin' ye wurr in the other."

MONEY IS SOMETIMES A MISFORTUNE.—There is something about money which dries up the affections. Perhaps one reason for this is that the moment people get any money there are so many trying to get it away from them that they think the whole human race are their enemies.

LET HIM READ HIS OWN WRITING.

The handwriting of the famous Scottish divine, Dr. Chalmers, was so very illegible that his fond mother used to say to her husband when a letter arrived from her son:—

"Juist lay it aside, and Tammas will read it to us himsel' when he comes home."

EVERY-DAY CHRISTIANITY.—Carry religion into common life, and your life will be rendered useful as well as noble. There are many women who listen incredulously to the high-toned exhortations of the pulpit: the religious life there depicted is much too seraphic, they think, for this plain and prosaic world of ours. Show these women that the picture is not a fancy one; make it a reality. Bring religion down from the clouds; apply it to the infallible test of experiment, and, by suffusing your daily actions with holy principles, prove that love to God, superiority to worldly pleasures, spirituality, holiness, heavenly-mindedness, are something more than the stock ideas of sermons.—*Caird.*

WHAT GOLDSMITH SAID.

"The modest virgin, the prudent wife, or the careful matron, are much more serviceable in life than petticoated philosophers, blustering heroines, or virago queens."

A REASON FOR LEAVING.

Lady: "Why did you leave your last place?"

Servant: "Well, you see, mum, I had to pay for all my breakages, and as they came to more than my wages, you see, mum, it was a kind of imposition that I couldn't stand."

RIDICULE MIGHT BE OF SOME SERVICE.—If ridicule were employed to laugh people out of vice and folly, it might be of some service; but it is too often made use of to laugh people out of virtue and good sense by attacking everything solemn and serious.

Further contributions to the Princess Louise Home:—

Rachel E. Daft, Lisbon, 1s.; E. N. N., 1s.; Miss F. Newbolt, annual subscription to "G. O. P." Convalescent Home, 1s.

PRECIOUS STONES; THEIR HOMES, HISTORIES. AND INFLUENCE.

By EMMA DREWER.

CHAPTER IV.

THE RUBY AND THE SAPPHIRE.—*Hardness, 9; Specific Gravity, 4.*

The ruby signifies divine power and love, dignity and royalty, while the blue-coloured sapphire is an emblem of heaven, virtue, truth, constancy, heavenly love and contemplation.

" The ruby doth cast forth the glory of its splendour and its sparklings like lightning."
Thos. Nicols, 1652.

" And there was under his feet as it were a paved work of a sapphire-stone, and as it were the body of heaven in his clearness."
Ex. xxiv. 10.

IN all the world and in every age there has been but one idea of a perfect ruby, *viz.*, that it is the most rare of all the productions of nature, that it forms the highest known standard of perfection, and excels in value the diamond itself.

When the ancients desired to convey the idea of something very precious they compared it with the ruby, for example, " The price of wisdom is above rubies," and " Who can find a virtuous woman ? for her price is above rubies."

It is not difficult to imagine that in the age of superstition wonderful qualities were ascribed to it, for whatever startle l the imagination of the ancients with a new and mysterious beauty was at once invested with supernatural power.

It was firmly believed that the ruby furnished light to certain great serpents or dragons whose eyes had become feeble through old age ; also that it had the power of shining brilliantly in darkness, and that its light was of such a nature that nothing could arrest it. It was a matter of firm faith that if the ruby were worn in an amulet it was good against poison and the plague, and that so worn it would drive away evil thoughts, sadness, bad dreams and wicked spirits ; it was also credited with the attribute of cheering the mind and keeping the body in safety, and even of warning the wearer of the approach of danger by growing black and obscure, and returning to its former colour when the danger was past. In fact the belief prevailed that the presiding genius of a man's fate might be carried with him in the shape of a ruby.

The following occurrence is related by Wolfgangus Gabelschoverus—

" This have I often heard from celebrated men of high estate and also know I it, woe is me! from my own experience ; for on the 5th day of December, 1600 after the birth of Christ Jesus, as I was going with my beloved wife, of pious memory, from Stutgard to Caluna I observed by the way that a very fine ruby which I wore mounted in a gold ring, the which she had given to me, lost repeatedly and almost completely its splendid colour, and that it assumed a sombre blackish hue which blackness lasted not one day but several : so much so that being greatly astonished I drew the ring from my finger and put it into a casket. I also warned my wife that some evil followed her or me, the which I augured from the change in the ruby. And truly I was not deceived, for within a few days she was taken

mortally sick. After her death the ruby resumed its pristine colour and brilliancy."

It was related by Sir John Maundeville, a traveller in the fourteenth century, who visited a royal court in the East, that the emperor had in his chamber pillars of gold, in one of which was a ruby or carbuncle of half a foot long which, in the night, gave so much light and shining as to be equal to the light of day ; and by Louis Verolam the story was told that the King of Pegu wore carbuncles of such a size and lustre that whoever looked at him in the dark saw him as resplendent as though he were illumined by the sun. It is related also in Ælian's *Book of Animals* that " a woman of the name of Heraclia, having cured a stork of a broken leg, the grateful bird brought and dropped into her bosom a carbuncle or true ruby which shone in the darkness of night like a lighted lamp."

Putting aside, however, all the quaint pretty stories, beliefs and mystic powers with which the fancies of a few thousand years have endowed precious stones, and this one specially, we come face to face with facts important for us to know, *viz.*, the composition, the home and surroundings of the ruby and the sapphire, which are one and the same stone varying only in colour.

These two stones do not always grow up together, and their colour is derived from their surroundings just as two children in a family exhibit different characteristics if brought up under different influences.

We have seen that the pearl is composed of lime and the diamond of pure carbon, therefore we shall not be unprepared to find that the ruby and the sapphire, exquisite as they are, are formed almost entirely of clay, a substance quite as common as lime and carbon.

It scarcely seems possible that the material with which children make mud pies can have anything in common with the ruby and the sapphire, but so it is.

The basis of clay is alumina, a substance which exists largely in vegetable mould and in most of the rocks of the world, and it is of alumina nearly pure that the ruby and the sapphire are formed. I say nearly pure, because some faint traces of foreign matter, such as oxide of iron or chromic acid are detected in them, and probably it is these minute particles coming into contact with the alumina which afford the colouring to these exquisite gems.

Just as we saw that the diamond had a double in an inferior variety, so the ruby has its inferior in the Oriental topaz, the first being a hundred times more valuable than the last. There exists but one true ruby, " of colour glorious and effects rare," and that is the Oriental ruby. When its colour is of good quality it has the tint of arterial blood, a tint known in commerce as " pigeon's blood." Some of the reds in the stained glass of our ancient cathedrals. when the daylight pours through, give an idea of this brilliant colour.

Formerly the people of the East called all coloured stones by the name of ruby, and in the language of Pegu, the sapphire was a blue ruby, the topaz a pink ruby, the amethyst a violet ruby, and so on.

The ruby, sometimes called carbuncle from its fiery appearance, is easily distinguished by a property shared by the sapphire and the emerald, and which is known as dichroism, and belongs only to those gems whose form is six-sided or pyramidal. The stones which possess this power, when viewed in different directions, exhibit two distinct colours—the ruby, aurora red and carmine ; the sapphire, greenish straw

and blue, the emerald, yellowish green and bluish green, while diamonds, garnets, and spinel, which crystallise in the cubic system, show a pair of images identical in colour.

The name given to all minerals consisting of alumina nearly pure, is corundum. This is very largely distributed over the world, but the fine red varieties are extremely rare ; indeed, it may be said that they have no home outside Burma, Siam, and Ceylon, and even of these it is only Burma which is celebrated for the favourite tint known as the true pigeon blood ; those of Siam being often too dark and those of Ceylon too light to satisfy the connoisseur.

It is only of late years that we have learnt anything definite about the home and surroundings of the ruby, and great thanks are due to Mr. Streeter, whose skill, energy, and organisation have opened up to us a mass of information respecting the character of the country in which rubies are found, and the working of the mines not only in Burma, but also in Montana.

As to the origin of the ruby little is known. Cardan, who was born in 1801, declared they were engendered by juices distilled from precious minerals, while the people of the East believed that rubies ripen in the earth ; that they are first colourless and crude, and gradually as they ripen become yellow, green, blue, and red, which they considered the highest point of beauty and ripeness. But to go from fancies to facts. The mines in which rubies are found are as a rule natural caverns into which ruby-sand and clay have been washed. They are also found in calc-spar, and it has been thought by some therefore that calc-spar is the matrix or mother-rock of the ruby, while others with more reason, perhaps, think that the calc-spar has closed round the gem, but whence the ruby itself originally came is a mystery up to the present time.

The knowledge that ruby mines existed in Burma first reached Europe in the fifteenth century, but there was so much mystery about them that up to the beginning of 1886, the date of the annexation of Upper Burma to the British Empire, we were quite ignorant as to the conditions under which these gems occurred in this inaccessible country. The mines were so strictly guarded that no European was allowed to approach them on any pretence. They were a royal monopoly, and fine stones could only be obtained for the outside world by smuggling, as the order was to retain all for the king's treasury. One of the titles of the King of Burma was " Lord of the Rubies." The origin of the king's possession of these mines is given in the following tradition.

In the year 1630 it happened that a Burman came to Mogok, a hundred miles north of Mandalay, with tamarinds for sale, and having obtained a red stone in exchange for some of his fruit presented it to the King of Ava, the ancient capital of Burma. The king was so pleased with the ruby that he entered into negotiations for the tract of country which produced such minerals, and in the year 1637 he peacefully obtained the ruby district in exchange for other territory, and from that time to this it is probable that the majority of fine rubies have come directly or indirectly from Upper Burma.

Since the ruby tract has been worked by Europeans, first by Mr. Streeter and now by the mining company, large numbers of rubies have been found, but most of them small, and not enough to pay the heavy rental, but great hopes are entertained that the coming years will be more successful.

country which is the chief centre of
y mining district is a dense mass of
jungle rising above the valleys, which
tivated for rice, and the climate is very
by both for Europeans and natives.
ines may be divided into three classes
pit, the hillside-working, and the
The first of these is worked in the
bottoms in dry weather; they seem to
s of former lakes gradually filled up by
s deposited there by successive rains.
d of *byòn*, or ruby-bearing earth, is at a
of from fifteen to twenty feet.
he wet season the working of the hill-
ittings commences; the *byòn* here is
:llowish-brown colour; the water for
g is often brought for miles along the
es by ditches, forming a large item of
:. The third class, or cave-workings,
y interesting, but attended with con-
le danger; the air, too, is so foul that
ften impossible to work or to keep
burning. The *byòn* here is of a more
ature than in either of the others, and
there are fewer stones found they are,
e, of better size and quality.
working tools of the Burmese miners
y simple. He has a rough dress to
the mine; his lamp is a little earthen-
ucer of oil, with a wick burning at one
or digging he has a spud shaped like a
wel, a few sprigs cut from the nearest
mboos to make a platform, and some
-stalks to serve as ropes; and then he
i he requires. The use of modern
ery and of explosives by Burmese
is prohibited by law.
public place of sale in Mandalay for
e of rubies is called Ruby Hall, and
lso as a kind of intelligence office. In
was estimated that the value of the
ent every month to the hall was between
and 100,000 rupees.
rever the ruby is found, there, as a
her stones of value may be seen; and
rubies and sapphires meet together it
taken as a fact that gold is not far off.
wo most important rubies ever known
pe were brought to England in 1875.
ere re-cut in London, and their colour
ignificent. One sold for £10,000 and
ger for £20,000. "It is doubtful,"
r. Streeter, "if the London market
ever bore seen these truly royal gems
the necessities of the late Burmese
ment." In Burma the sale of these
jies caused intense excitement, a mili-
ird being considered necessary to escort
rsons conveying the package to the

on is the most marvellous gem deposit
rorld, and was known in the period of
nan empire as the land of the luminous
le; but, as more sapphires are found
an rubies, we will speak of it in the
rt of this chapter.

THE SAPPHIRE.

azure light of sapphire stone
embles that celestial throne,
ymbol of each simple heart
t grasps in hope the better part,
ere life each holy deed combines,
in the light of virtue shines."
Marbodeus.

sapphire has been known from earliest
y, and venerated beyond all other
s stones; indeed, it was known to the
i as the sacred stone, and was en-
by them with the most exalted quali-
: was one of the gems which had
Aaron's breastplate, and was chosen
ems to represent the throne of God.
es states that the vision which ap-
to Moses on the mount was in a
:, and that the first tables of the law
r God to Moses were also of sapphire.

It is supposed to have been the earliest gem
known to man; and long before the diamond,
with its less attractive natural appearance,
was recognised as valuable, the bright-coloured
ruby and sapphire caught the eyes of the early
inhabitants of the earth as the stones were
separated from the matrix and laid bare by
the mountain torrents.
Specimens of sapphire are found among the
ruins of the ancient and long-forgotten cities
of Arabia and Persia, where one looks in vain
for diamonds. This is not surprising, seeing
that the diamond was unnoticed and unknown
until civilisation, far advanced, revealed its
hidden splendour by the application of art.
All precious stones have, it is believed, an
antipathy to vice and intemperance, but the
sapphire, above all others, has this quality.
If worn by a person of bad habits, it never
displays its full beauty, and it is stated as a
reason why it is specially worn by priests that
it helps the wearer to be pure in thought and
deed. And so great was its power supposed
to be on venomous creatures that if a sapphire
were placed over the mouth of a phial containing a spider the insect died on the instant.
It was an article of belief that powdered
sapphires, made into a paste and placed over
the eyes, would draw out any dust, insect, or
other foreign matter that may have fallen into
and injured them.
The sapphire, in its purest state, is of a
clear blue colour, very much like that of the
blossom of the cornflower, and the more
velvety its appearance the greater its value.
Although more widely distributed over the
earth than its sister the ruby, it is no more
lavish in its production of the true cornflower
blue, which is the standard colour, than the
ruby of its pigeon-blood colour.
Wherever perfect sapphires are found, their
home or mother is ferruginous sand (that is,
containing iron), produced by decomposition
of basaltic rock.
In former times Europe obtained sapphires
almost entirely from Arabia, and subsequently
from Persia and Ceylon. At present, the
best sapphire-yielding localities are Burma,
Cashmir, Siam, Ceylon, and, quite lately,
Montana, but of all these Siam produces the
finest. The stones yielded by these mines
are of the highly-prized velvety blue colour,
and fortunately those over one carat in weight
are better in colour and quality than those
under. Although these mines have only been
worked about a quarter of a century, they
must have been known long ago by the
natives. They consist of rude pits, about four
feet square and five to twelve feet deep, on
the sides of the mountain and in the valley.
The stratum in which the sapphires are here
found is clay with a small admixture of gravel.
The miners, chiefly Burmese, work two or
three in a pit, and raise the sapphire-earth
in baskets by means of ropes made with
creepers.
The clay is then washed and the gems
picked out of the residuum by hand. The
curious habit obtains here of not allowing the
buyer to see the sapphires before purchasing;
the stones are put into a short joint of a small
bamboo, and the intending purchaser judges
of their weight by the rattle they make when
shaken.
The great gem-bearing district of Siam is
supposed to cover an area of a hundred square
miles. So extensive is the trade in Siamese
sapphires, that a gem broker in London
certified that in 1889 he sold wholesale nearly
£70,000 worth of these stones.
In Upper Burma, sapphires are found
associated with rubies, and although not of
very fine quality they are of large size. The
largest ever found in Burma weighed 253 carats,
and was purchased for the king for 7000
rupees.
About thirteen years ago a remarkable dis-

covery was made in the valley of the Hima-
layas in Cashmere. It seems that a landslip
occurred about the year 1880 and laid bare the
rock exposing sapphires. The surrounding
rocks are of gneiss and crystalline limestone
intersected by veins of granite. The sapphires
were found loose among the detritus on the
side of the valley high up the mountain near
the line of perpetual snow. This first supply
soon came to an end, but a second landslip
having occurred fresh deposits have been exposed. Some of these Cashmere sapphires are
of very fine colour. Here, as in many of the other
findings of precious stones, a true and interesting story is attached.* Near the spot where
the sapphires have been found lived a monk,
who first noticed a pale blue vein in the rock.
He broke off pieces and exchanged them with
traders for sugar and tobacco, carefully con-
cealing whence he obtained his treasures. Subsequently he disposed of a quantity to some
men who took the pieces to Simla. One
piece, about a foot long and three or four inches
in circumference, he was persuaded to give to
one of his brotherhood in order to have an
idol made of it. A lapidary engaged to
form it into the idol found it so hard that he
came to the conclusion it was of extraordinary
value, and showed it to an official, who decided
to send it to the Maharajah of Cashmere.
On enquiry being made a messenger was
despatched to bring the monk who had found
the stone, and he was compelled to disclose the
locality where he had obtained it. The result
was, that a responsible official with a strong
guard was sent to protect the place until the
value of the discovery should be known.
Sapphires are found by the Lucba Pass,
which is about ten days' journey from Simla. A
native is said to have found a large number
here, and loading several goats with these
valuables he took the journey to Simla where
he tried to sell them; but the people to whom
he showed them knew nothing of their value,
and would not give even a rupee for them,
which the man would gladly have taken, for he
was starving. He then proceeded to Delhi,
where the jewellers, knowing them to be
sapphires, gave him their value and bad them
cut and sent to London.
In Ceylon, the sapphires are usually found
with other gems either in the old river-beds or in
a bed of gravel which occurs at a depth of from
six to twenty feet below the surface.
The gem mart of Ceylon, Ratnapoora,
which means literally the city of rubies, is
situate in the very midst of the mines, and the
beds of the torrents sometimes contain so great
a quantity of broken fragments of sapphire,
garnet and other stones, that the sands are
often used by the lapidaries in polishing gems.
It is the opinion of learned men that the
sapphire is formed in crystalline rocks; that
in process of time the matrix, or mother-rock,
is disintegrated, the gems set free, and washed
down to the alluvial soils where they are now
found.
The sapphire-mines of Montana are, says
Mr. Streeter, after visiting them, exceedingly
rich both in precious stones and gold. The
existence of curious stones in North Carolina
and Montana territory has long been known;
they were seen by the gold-mining pioneers,
who, when they tried to get an opinion upon
them, were told they were merely specimens
of quartz. On leaving Montana for what they
supposed richer fields, some took a few of the
stones away with them, which falling into
the hands of Messrs. Tiffany, jewellers of New
York, were recognised as true sapphires and
rubies.
The most important sapphires known in
Europe are two magnificent stones, which
were exhibited in the London Exhibition of
1862 and in the Paris Exhibition of 1867.

* Related in Streeter's *Precious Stones and Gems.*

The smaller of the two was perhaps the more valuable; it was a badly-shaped stone, but when re-cut in London and all defects removed it was a splendid gem of 165 carats, and worth from £7000 to £8000.

In the Hope Collection there was a large sapphire of a rich colour, which retained its beauty as well by candle as by daylight.

Among the jewels of the Baroness Burdett-Coutts are two magnificent sapphires, said to be worth £30,000.

Among celebrated sapphires is the one found in Bengal by a poor man who sold wooden spoons. It is over 133 carats in weight, and is without spot or fault. It was brought to Europe and bought by the house of Raspoli in Rome. Later it became the property of a German prince, who sold it to the French jewel-merchant Perret for £6800. It forms one of a collection in the Jardin des Plantes in Paris.

The ancients engraved the sapphire, notwithstanding its hardness, and a beautiful specimen of this may be seen among the Crown jewels of Russia, representing a female figure enveloped in drapery. The stone is of two tints, and the artist has made use of the dark tint for the woman and the light for the drapery. Another specimen in the Stroz Cabinet in Rome is a perfect marvel of skill representing a young Hercules.

We have now disposed of those gems whose composition is carbonate of lime (the pearl pure carbon (the diamond), and clay, the bas of which is alumina (ruby and sapphire); and it would be difficult to say which of all these common materials have turned out, with the help of mother Nature, the most perfect and exquisite gem.

MERMAIDENS.

By SARAH TYTLER, Author of "A Young Oxford Maid," etc.

CHAPTER XIV.

WITH the first streaks of dawn and the first lull in the gale so that it was possible to put the damaged gig to sea, Tom launched her afresh. He took no more men than were needed to row her, for although there was no lack of volunteers for the task, it was at the imminent risk of their lives they went in such a sea. The boat was already leaking, so that it was with difficulty the water could be bailed out of her fast enough to keep her from sinking within a few furlongs of the reef.

We girls had seen Tom and Perry consulting together before the gig started, and we could guess why one went and the other stayed. Somebody belonging to us must be left with us, else if the boat were swamped (ah, me, what an if!) our plight would be still more pitiable. I believe Perry waived his claim as senior to command the boat and start with his life in his hand, because Tom was father's son, and who had so good a right as the son to go to the help of the father?

It was a forlorn hope—more forlorn than we suspected at the time, for we were not aware that, with the morning light, no sign could be detected, through the one glass which remained to us, of the ship which had been visible from the reef on the previous evening. She might have drifted beyond the range of the glass, or as was more probable she might have gone down in the night; but while there was the smallest chance of her survival, or of the existence of any of her crew Tom felt it incumbent on him to do something, and God was merciful, as He always is, even when He smites. After these series of disasters He sent us three crowning mercies. The sea and the wind fell as they had not done from the beginning of the storm, in a shorter time than we could have dared to hope. The battered gig lived as by a miracle, and Tom brought back in her, oh, joy beyond reckoning, father alive and unhurt as a salvage from the wreck. The Sea Serpent had, indeed, put the finishing touch to her catalogue of misfortunes by sinking like a stone before the night was ended; but she had not done so without giving, like the good ship she was, timely warning of what was going to happen. The hastily repaired jolly-boat was launched by the light of the ship lanterns, with the idea of simply keeping her afloat till morning broke; but seeing how inadequate the boat was to take off all the men in the ship, father absolutely refused to go with her. He was on the deck of the Sea Serpent when she went down. How he escaped being sucked down with her—like most of the men, only the All-seeing could tell. Father was seen by the light of a ship lantern in the jolly-boat, struggling with the waves, and was picked up by the men. Then followed such an experience as few survived to tell. The jolly-boat shipped seas enough to have swamped a boat of thrice its size and in perfect condition. It was tossed and whirled in the leaping, bounding, surging water. Even after it had endured till morning, even after Tom had sighted it and was rowing hard towards it, the jolly-boat capsized; and when aid reached it, the boat was floating keel upmost, and only father and his old boatswain were clinging to the keel! The other men, most of them younger by more than a score of years, had been swept away; only a handful, and among them three weak women, remained of the company of brave officers and able-bodied seamen who had constituted the crew of the Sea-Serpent. We could not think of the heavy loss just at that moment, but you must not imagine that we forgot and did not mourn in time for the familiar weather-beaten faces, the strong hands and kind hearts, the youth and manhood in their spring-time and their prime, whose sudden destruction was a drain on the forces of the country and an irreparable blow dealt to many a quiet island home, far from the sound of the sea.

We were humbly thankful for the lives which were spared to us, and were eager to do the utmost to help each other in our sore strait.

It was a sight to see: that meeting between father and Jane. How determined he was to persuade her that he had been in no danger to speak of during the past night, and how resolute she was to convince him that she was as well as possible and was suffering no inconvenience from sitting or lying on a damp mattress in a leaky tent, with only a barren rock and a tumbling sea within sight.

We could now, when our attention was undisturbed, take a review of our situation and sum up our possessions such as they were. We could expect nothing more from our dear old ship with all its home comforts, except such poor jetsam and flotsam as the sea might bring with in our reach, so that we might dismiss our first and most natural resource from our thoughts. We were about twenty men and women in all, and our resource amounted to how much? To nothing in the way of live stock; such as we had owned had perished, and even the cattle cases of cows and sheep were never cast on the reef; some contrary current carried them in another direction. We had a few barrels of undamaged biscuit flour and pork, casks with water, a boat with wine and a case of spirits, these were literally all our stores, and they would hardly last us ten days, supposing the we were dealt out in famine rations, while we were equally out of the track of ship bound for the Cape or for Australasia. Our only boat, light at the best, had sustained such damage that when she was once more drawn up on the reef, she was found, to the consternation of the beholders, to be falling to pieces. To venture to sea in her again in the state she was in would be to court the death from which we had narrowly escaped and, alas! though we had amateur carpenters in plenty, we had neither proper materials, nor tools with which to "cobble" the boat in the roughest fashion.

The reef was at first glance destitute of provision for human life. We need not fear the springing out upon us from secret lurking-places of such cannibals and savages as Susie's head had been full of. No such luck as the discovery of a devoted "Friday" was likely to befall us. It was a deficiency to which we were the more easily reconciled, since modern specimen of the faithful black man would have implied another mout to fill, while we had no need of farther company. At the same time the opportunity of making the acquaintance of brand new unsophisticated member of the aborigines would not have lost its charm even yet for Jane. There was no possibility of a secret lurking-place on the reef. Perry and Tom traversed it from end to end in a day and a half. It was, as I have described it, a bare ridge of rock with just the nucleus of land

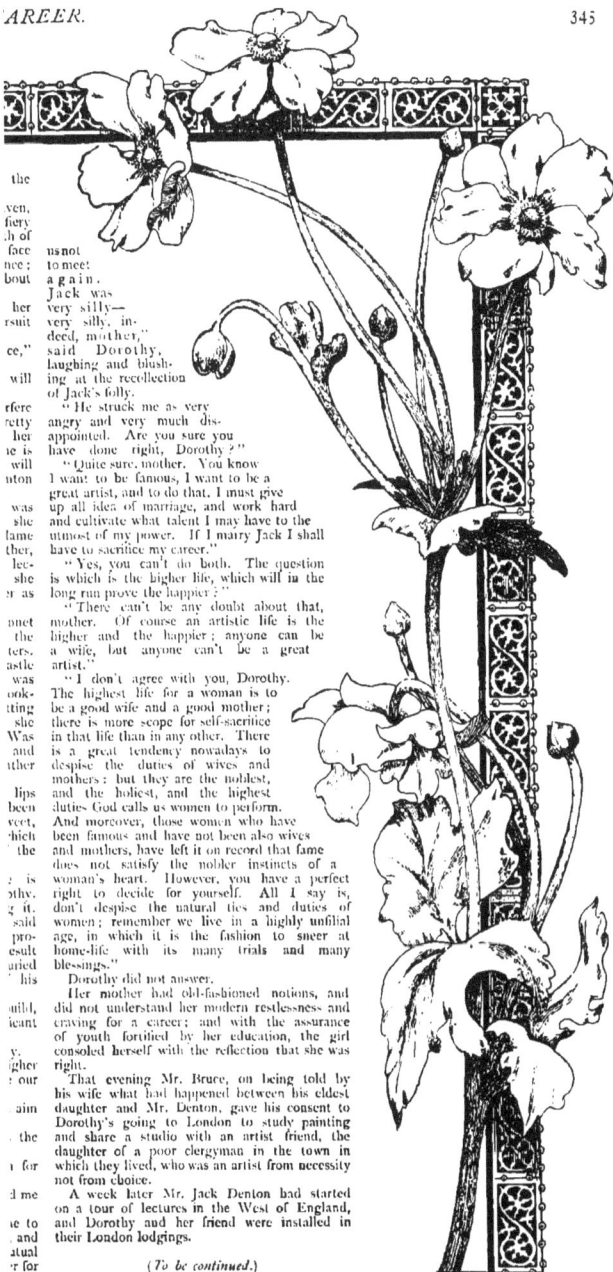

the
ven,
fiery
ch of
face
nce ;
bout

her
rsuit

ce,"

will

rfere
retty
her
ie is
will
nton

was
she
fame
ther,
lec-
she
er as

onet
the
ters.
astle
was
ook-
tting
she
Was
and
ither

lips
been
veet,
which
the

: is
othy.
g it.
said
pro-
esult
aried
his

uild,
icant

y.
igher
: our

aim

the

i for

d me

ie to
, and
atual
r for

us not
to meet
again.
Jack was
very silly—
very silly, in-
deed, mother,"
said Dorothy,
laughing and blush-
ing at the recollection
of Jack's folly.

"He struck me as very
angry and very much dis-
appointed. Are you sure you
have done right, Dorothy?"

"Quite sure, mother. You know
I want to be famous, I want to be a
great artist, and to do that, I must give
up all idea of marriage, and work hard
and cultivate what talent I may have to the
utmost of my power. If I marry Jack I shall
have to sacrifice my career."

"Yes, you can't do both. The question
is which is the higher life, which will in the
long run prove the happier?"

"There can't be any doubt about that,
mother. Of course an artistic life is the
higher and the happier; anyone can be
a wife, but anyone can't be a great
artist."

"I don't agree with you, Dorothy.
The highest life for a woman is to
be a good wife and a good mother;
there is more scope for self-sacrifice
in that life than in any other. There
is a great tendency nowadays to
despise the duties of wives and
mothers: but they are the noblest,
and the holiest, and the highest
duties God calls us women to perform.
And moreover, those women who have
been famous and have not been also wives
and mothers, have left it on record that fame
does not satisfy the nobler instincts of a
woman's heart. However, you have a perfect
right to decide for yourself. All I say is,
don't despise the natural ties and duties of
women; remember we live in a highly unfilial
age, in which it is the fashion to sneer at
home-life with its many trials and many
blessings."

Dorothy did not answer.

Her mother had old-fashioned notions, and
did not understand her modern restlessness and
craving for a career; and with the assurance
of youth fortified by her education, the girl
consoled herself with the reflection that she was
right.

That evening Mr. Bruce, on being told by
his wife what had happened between his eldest
daughter and Mr. Denton, gave his consent to
Dorothy's going to London to study painting
and share a studio with an artist friend, the
daughter of a poor clergyman in the town in
which they lived, who was an artist from necessity
not from choice.

A week later Mr. Jack Denton had started
on a tour of lectures in the West of England,
and Dorothy and her friend were installed in
their London lodgings.

(To be continued.)

ALL ABOUT THE EMERALD.

By EMMA BREWER.

" The emerald burns intensely bright,
With radiance of an olive light ;
This is the faith that highest shines,
No need of charity declines,
And seeks no rest and shuns no strife
In working out a holy life."

TRANGELY curious are the traditions concerning emeralds, and the way they have been guarded from falling into the hands of man. It seems as though the spirit of evil recognised the purifying influence of these stones upon the human race, and therefore put every possible obstacle in the way of those who sought them. And oddly enough the belief that demons, griffins and wicked spirits guard the emerald mines, wherever they may be, is as potent in this nineteenth century as in times gone by. A miraculous solution of the origin of emeralds is given in Forbes' *Oriental Memoirs.* "A person was watching a swarm of fire-flies in an Indian grove one moonlight night. After hovering for a time in the moonbeams one particular fire-fly more brilliant than the rest alighted on the grass and there remained. The spectator struck by its fixity, and approaching to ascertain the cause, found not an insect but an emerald, which he appropriated and wore in a ring."

We have not yet discovered those African mines whence the ancients drew their splendid stones, and the first we have any account of are those in Scythia, where the finest Oriental emeralds were said to have their home in gold mines. But they might almost as well not have existed so impossible was it for man to force an entrance. Access to them was strictly guarded, so goes the account, by ferocious griffins who built their nests there, and who were constantly at work in the bowels of the earth searching for gold and emeralds, which having found they would hide and never give up to ordinary mortals. So the only thing to be done was to apply for help to a nation of pigmy Cyclops, a people with only one eye, and that in their forehead, whose home was in Scythia, near the river with golden sands, and whose occupation was to wage war against their natural enemies the griffins, monstrous animals that robbed them of the gold of their river and the emeralds of their mines.

These fictions were testified to as facts by Pliny and Strabo and other well known authorities ; it is therefore no wonder that the mystery which enveloped the finding of the emerald should so long have remained undispelled.

Only a little more than seventy years ago when Monsieur Caillard was working the Mount Zebarah emerald mines in Egypt, he discovered that the superstitious fears and fancies which had ruled the people of long ago were now fully possessed by the Arabs, a deputation of whom waited upon him in order to caution him against sleeping near the emerald caves, as they were the refuge of snakes, wolves, and other beasts of prey, and more especially the abode of demons who would resent his intrusion.

Stevenson, in his *Residence in South America*, vol. ii., also bears witness to this feeling. Speaking of the emerald mine in the neighbourhood of " Las Esmeraldas," he says, " I never visited it owing to the superstitious

dread of the natives, who assured me that it was enchanted and guarded by a dragon which poured forth thunder and lightning on those who dared ascend the river."

There can be no doubt that emeralds were known in remote ages, for necklaces of these beautiful stones have been discovered in Etruscan tombs, at Herculaneum and at Pompeii, as well as in the excavations of old Rome.

Evidently the ancient Egyptians used the emerald largely, for M. Caillard discovered the caves and mines in which they worked ; and some of them were so large that four hundred men could work side by side ; he found ropes, lamps, levers and tools of many kinds which they had evidently employed. Many fine emeralds have come from Siberia ; the first of them was found accidentally in 1830 by a charcoal burner at the root of a tree on the east side of the Ural.

The Tyrolean Alps are rich in emeralds although there is no systematic working of them. Near Salzburg, for example, they are found embedded in mica slate in the sides of two tall perpendicular rocks, which are so steep as to be inaccessible except to the very few, who, willing to risk their lives, choose to let themselves down by means of ropes or *seilen* and remain suspended over the frightful chasm while they detach the emeralds with their tools. Among those who have thus ventured is a woman, who had her reward in the number of fine emeralds she secured.

For the last two centuries and more our finest emeralds have come from Peru. They are superior in colour to the African : their tints are purer, and they have less of foreign matter, which is apt to render the reflection variable. Those taken from Mount Zebarah by M. Caillard were of a pale green colour, cloudy and full of flaws. They are well-known in Cairo and Constantinople, where they are perforated for earrings. The harness of the Sultan's horses is covered with emeralds of this kind taken from Egyptian mines. The finest emeralds are of a very fine dark velvety green, and these are more frequently found in the Muzo mines north-west of Santa Fé. They are worked by a company who pay an annual rent of 24,000 dollars to the Republic of Columbia.

The great Muzo mine is a sort of tunnel of about one hundred yards deep, with very inclined walls. Mr. Streeter says that on the summit of the mountains and quite near to the mouth of the mine are large lakes shut off by means of water-gates, which can be easily shifted when the miners require water. The matrix of the emerald is here a sort of pitchy limestone rich in carbon and embedded in red sandstone and clay slate. " To obtain the emeralds," Mr. Streeter continues, " the workmen begin by cutting steps on the inclined walls of the mine in order to get firm resting-places for their feet. The overseer places the men at certain distances from each other to cut a wide step with the help of pickaxes. The loosened stones fall by their own weight to the bottom of the mine. When this begins to fill, a sign is given to let the waters loose. These rush down with great vehemence, carrying the fragments of rock with them through the mountain into the basin. This operation is repeated until the beds are exposed in which the emeralds lie. The stones are sometimes accompanied by beautiful crystals of iron pyrites. Sometimes an emerald is found in fragments, which when placed together form one beautiful crystal. Again it is not an unusual thing for the

emerald to break after its separation from the matrix or home, but this can be prevented by placing the stones in a vessel for some days, and protecting them from the rays of the sun."

The emeralds occur in pockets, therefore the mining may for some time be unprofitable and disheartening, when suddenly the reward comes in a discovery of good stones.

It may be a matter of surprise that India, to which we naturally turn as the home of all things rare and beautiful, was not entrusted by mother nature with the housing and care of the emerald, which is a gem of high personal character, subtle and exquisite colour, and possessing ennobling and healing virtues. India loves it and imports it, but has not the honour of producing it. It has, however, the credit of naming it—the origin of emerald being a Sanskrit word signifying green—the root of the word in Eastern tongues means a something that waves about like a bright green seaweed.

How the emerald came by its beautiful colour is far from being perfectly understood, notwithstanding all that science has taught us. There is nothing for it but to take M. Babinet's advice, which is " to admire without penetrating the secret of the unparalleled red of the ruby, the pure yellow of the topaz, the unmingled greenness of the emerald, the soft blue of the sapphire, and the rich violet of the amethyst, and be content to leave the unravelling of the mystery to posterity."

Of course the age in which we live is not barren of suggestions or lacking in opinions as to the colouring of the emerald. According to some scientific men it is derived from the decomposition of animals which have lived in a bygone age and whose remains are now found fossilised in the rock which forms the home of this precious stone, while others are of opinion that the colour is due to oxide of chromium.

When an emerald is possessed of a tint of beautiful quality it is one of the rarest and most precious of stones and valued at a quarter above that of the diamond of like size. It is so rare that few have ever seen a full-sized perfect emerald. The following anecdote will show the value set upon it and why.

It is related by a physician that his brother, a jeweller, received of Francescus Maria Prince of Urbine a very large sum of money to buy him an emerald, of the weight of eight grains of wheat, most pure and Oriental, that by it he might receive alleviation in an infirmity with which he was troubled withal.

A bishop writing A.D. 640, says, " The emerald surpasses in its greenness all green stones and even the leaves of plants, and imparts to the air around it a green shimmer, and its colour is most soothing to the eyes of those engaged in cutting and polishing the stone."

Pliny recognised it as being refreshing to weak eyes. " If," he says, " the sight hath been wearied and dimmed by intentive poring upon anything else, beholding of this stone doth refresh and restore it again."

Before we go into the interesting subject of the mysterious properties of the emerald, which have endeared it to the rich and wise in all ages, we must look into the matter of its composition and observe of what materials mother nature has formed it. For seeing how many and great powers were appointed to guard its exit from home, it must surely be made of superior materials to those with which she formed the pearl, the diamond, and the ruby. And yet we are not surprised on the whole to find that if she could make pearls of lime, diamonds of carbon, and rubies of clay, she could have no difficulty in forming emeralds out of sand or silica, and this is exactly what she has done with the help of a little alumina and glucina. This last is a rare substance, and up to this time has only been found in the emerald and two other stones; it is distinguished from other earths by its sweetness. Chemists say that the greater the quantity of glucina in an emerald the deeper is its green tint.

Silica, or sand, which forms the basis of the emerald, is used in many other ways; it is a chief ingredient in all kinds of glass, from the "green bottle" to the plate and flint glass. It is the peculiar treatment that these common materials receive which raises them to the aristocracy of precious stones. It seems to us scarcely possible that the silver sand used in our kitchens and sculleries can have anything in common with the exquisite and valuable emerald.

Just as the precious stones we have already noticed have their doubles in an inferior variety, so the emerald has close relationship with the beryl and aquamarine, which are practically the same mineral, though with certain differences. To the chemist, these may be trivial, but to the jeweller they are most important, as the one is almost priceless, while the others, although most attractive, can scarcely be reckoned as valuable. One great distinguishing mark is the colour, which in the emerald is a perfect green that seems to flash upon the surrounding objects and is unsurpassed by any other gem, whilst that of the beryl is yellow, and that of the aquamarine, a light-blue or sea-green, probably due to the presence of a small quantity of oxide of iron. The system of crystallisation is the same in all three, viz., hexagonal or six-sided prisms.

An emerald of a deep rich grass-green, clear and free from flaws, is worth from £20 to £40 a carat, while that of a lighter shade is worth much less, varying from 5s. to £15 a carat.

No other gem has been counterfeited with such perfection as the emerald, and it is sometimes almost impossible to distinguish the artificial from the real by the aid of the eye alone. One of the treasures forming part of Alaric's spoils in the 6th century was what is known in history as King Solomon's emerald table. It is described by enthusiastic Arab writers as a marvel of beauty, being formed of a single slab of solid emerald encircled with three rows of fine pearls, and supported on 365 feet of gold and gems. It is probably a specimen of the ingenuity of the glass workers of Tyre or Alexandria, and not a true emerald as it was believed to be. No doubt a great ignorance prevails about precious stones among the wearers and owners: as a proof the following is related by A. H. Church, Esq.

"A jeweller was showing a customer a bracelet beautifully set with green garnets of Bobrowska. The lady admired the stones and workmanship immensely, but spoke of the stones as emeralds. The jeweller, who was honest, said 'they are not emeralds, but a rare sort of garnet from the Ural mountains.' 'Well, after all,' said the lady, 'I don't very much care for this bracelet; show me another.' Not that she knew of any real objection to these garnets, which is that they are not quite hard enough to stand wear and tear."

The true emerald became much less rare in Europe after the conquest of Peru. The Spaniards possessed themselves of the hoards which had been increasing for centuries in the hands of the priests of the goddess Esmeralda, who was supposed to dwell in an emerald of the shape and size of an ostrich egg. These priests persuaded the people that the goddess esteemed the offering of emeralds higher than any other, and so on fêtes and holy days immense numbers were brought by the worshippers as devotional offerings.

Although a great many of these were ignorantly broken by the conquerors, Cortez was able to present a hundredweight of emeralds to the King of Spain, besides several of exquisite and rare beauty which he gave to his bride on her marriage with him, and which created envy in the heart of the Queen of Spain and his loss of favour at court.

There can be no doubt that emeralds were known and venerated in remote ages. It was the fourth of the gems mentioned in the Bible as worn in the breastplate of the high priest. They are mentioned in the 27th Chapter of Ezekiel: "Syria was thy merchant by reason of the multitude of wares of thy making; they occupied thy fairs with emerald, purple and broidered work, fine linen, agate and coral." The emerald is mentioned also in Rev. xxi. 19, as the fourth foundation of the New Jerusalem, and again in the 4th chapter and 3rd verse, where the rainbow of the New Covenant is spoken of as like unto an emerald, ever precious, beautiful, and refreshing.

The emerald held a very high place in the esteem of the ancients: it represented to them hope in immortality, exalted faith and victory over sin, and was endowed by them with very high attributes. It was an old Hebrew tradition that if a snake or serpent fixed its eye upon the lustre of the emerald, it immediately became blind. Thus Moore in "Lalla Rookh" says,

"Blinded like serpents, when they gaze
Upon the emerald's virgin blaze."

It was supposed to possess powerful medicinal qualities. Taken internally, it was considered a cure for venomous bites, fever and leprosy; if powerless to cure the evil, it shivered into atoms; applied to the lips it was declared to stop hemorrhage; worn round the neck, it dispelled vain terrors, was a restorer of sight and memory, and brought victory to the wearer. It was a firm belief that it taught the knowledge of secrets and future events. It is wonderful how these little bits of stones became endowed with such extraordinary virtues!

Objects were supposed to appear in a more favourable light when seen through an emerald, which explains why Nero used one when looking at the combats of the gladiators. It was an old belief that he who dreamed of green gems would become renowned and meet with truth and fidelity, while on the other hand, the falling of an emerald from its setting was regarded as an ill-omen to the wearer, and this last superstition obtains even in our day.

When George III. was crowned, a large emerald fell from his crown. America was lost in his reign, and was considered by many to have been thus foreshadowed.

When the tomb of Charlemagne at Aix-la-Chapelle was opened his bones were enveloped in Roman vestments, and round his neck, attached to a large chain of gold links, there hung a talisman consisting of a piece of the true cross and a beautiful emerald. The burghers of Aix-la-Chapelle presented it to Napoleon when he entered that town in 1811. One day in playful mood he threw it over the neck of Queen Hortense, declaring that he had worn it on his breast at battles as he supposed Charlemagne had done before him. From that day she never laid aside the precious relic.

Queen Elizabeth sent to Henry IV., the champion of the reformed faith, a beautiful emerald which she herself had worn. She gave it as a token of esteem, and reminded him that the gem possessed the virtue of not breaking so long as faith remained firm and entire.

The superstitious beliefs concerning the emerald suggested to Miss Landon the following beautiful lines—

" It is the gem which hath the power to show
If plighted lovers keep their faith or no;
If faithful, it is like the leaves of spring,
If faithless, like those leaves when withering.

Take back again your emerald gem,
There is no colour in the stone;
It might have graced a diadem,
But now its hue and light are gone.

Take back your gift and give me mine,
The kiss that sealed our last love vow;
Ah, other lips have been on thine,
My kiss is lost and sullied now!

The gem is pale, the kiss forgot,
And more than either you are changed;
But my true love has altered not,
My heart is broken, not estranged."

Very few engraved emeralds have descended to us from ancient times. This is not due to the hardness of the stone, but that it was evidently exempted on account of its beauty and great value. There is one, however, in the Devonshire gems of great antiquity and of great value, a large emerald cut into a gorgon's head in high relief.

Another with a history was the ring belonging to Polycrates, B.C. 530, which he was induced to throw into the sea as an offering to the gods for forty years of prosperity. It was an exquisite emerald, and he grieved over the loss of it; but a few days later he received a present of a large fish in which his ring was found.

The Shah of Persia has a little casket of gold studded with emeralds which is said to have been blessed by Mahomet, and has the property of rendering the royal wearer invisible as long as he remains unmarried.

The emerald was formerly much used for ornaments of dress and carriages. At the famous marriage-feast of Alexander and his eighty companions with their beautiful Persian brides, emeralds seem to have been the favourite gem worn, and to have been esteemed above all other ornaments except the beautiful pearls of the Persian Gulf. Pliny says that Paulina at the banquet was literally covered with emeralds and pearls in alternate rows.

Queen Elizabeth used precious stones almost recklessly. On the occasion of her visit to Tilbury a contemporary poet wrote—

" He happy was that could but see her coach,
The sides whereof beset with emeralds
And diamonds, with sparkling rubies red
In checkerwise by strange invention
With curious knots embroidered with gold."

In the fabulous life of Alexander the Great, printed towards the close of the 15th century, the hero found in the palace of the vanquished monarch many and great treasures, among which was a vine having its branches of gold, its leaves of emeralds, and its fruit of other precious stones.

THE WARDS OF ST. MARGARET'S.

CHAPTER II.
STARTING WORK.

"Is it not just as we take it,
This mystical world of ours?
Life's field will yield as we make it
A harvest of thorns or flowers."
Alice Cary.

BY SISTER JOAN.

HOSPITAL is situated south-west, not far from the Abbey and within easy distance of Saint James's Park. It is by no means one of the largest of which London can boast, and like many others is kept up chiefly by subscriptions. It possesses a medical school, and for many years before the time of which we are speaking has been the means of alleviating much suffering, by giving skilled aid and many comforts to those who would have sought vainly for either in their own homes. Many an aged man or woman found rest within its walls. Those who were brought in suffering from the effects of accidents or from acute forms of disease were promptly and skilfully tended. Children, too, of all ages were admitted, from babies of a few weeks old, and many who had had but little love at home (if home the place could be called where they were ushered into the world) found love and sympathy here. Tears were often shed at parting from nurse, who had been to the child almost a mother. Heartrending, indeed, would be the stories the wards might reveal could they but speak and relate the varying circumstances which brought each occupant to his bed. Sickness, sorrow, poverty, aye, and often sin would make up much of the tale, whilst death, that last dread visitant, would again and again close the record.

The day's work was over as far as most of the medical students were concerned, and they might be seen in groups in the hall, talking with eager voices before they separated. A four-wheeler stopped outside the flight of steps leading to the hospital, and stood unnoticed until a peal from the hall-bell directed every eye to the door.

"Here's another case for you, Ashton," said a fair-haired youth who was possessed of a slight amount of moustache and had the appearance at least of being more elderly than some of the number, to a tall dark man who was passing by. The voices, however, ceased as a cabman with a neat bullock trunk on his shoulder, followed by a young lady, simply dressed, entered the hall.

"Here you be. Miss," he said, "this be Saint Margaret's 'Orspital," and down went the box. The girl looked shy and confused, and turned to the porter who had come in answer to the bell, saying—

"I am a new nurse, can you tell me where I shall find the matron?"

"Oh," said he, "but you don't live here, you lives in the nusses' home, and that's just round the corner. You will find the matron there now," and after telling the cabman where to go, stood and watched them down the steps.

"A new probationer," said one. "I wonder what she'll be like?" "Going to make up to her," said another? "Well," said a third, "I hope she won't be put with King George. My! isn't it thundery there in a morning, sometimes!"

The cab with its tired occupant meanwhile crossed a square and stopped in front of a large building with a door possessed of a brass plate on which was engraved, "Home for Nurses." There can be no doubt, thought Constance, about this being the right place, and evidently the cabman shared her thought, for instead of questioning her as to whether he should ring or ask if he was right, as he had done at the hospital, he dismounted from his box, and running up a short flight of steps rang the bell with some force, saying kindly as he opened the door for her to alight, "Right this time, miss."

A servant in a print dress opened the door, and in reply to Constance's inquiry said the matron was in, but that she was engaged; however, she was expected and had best go at once to her room. When the man was paid and the great hall-door closed, Constance felt very much like running away; but she tried to feel brave, and was preparing to follow the servant, when she turned and said,

"I guess you'd like your things up with you, and if you take one side I don't mind giving you a hand with it, and you can jest 'ne settling yourself in," she added, not unkindly.

Constance thankfully accepted the offer in spite of a feeling of surprise at being expected to assist herself in carrying her luggage to her room. She took the handle at one end as she was told, and followed the servant at a brisk pace up two flights of stone stairs and along a passage with doors at each side, and on each door a number. Thirty-two stood ajar, and the servant pushed it open and entered. "This is your room," she said, as she put down the box. "When matron's disengaged I'll just let her know as how you've come, and she'll sure to see you. Tea is at five, and it only wants a quarter." So saying, she departed.

Constance looked round her little room. What was it that made a great lump rise in her throat? Possibly the memory of her own little sanctum at home. She was also tired and very cold. This is very much smaller than the servant's room at home, she said to herself, and just a tiny strip of carpet by the bed. How cheerless the bare boards look! Certainly the little bed was made, and very clean and comfortable it appeared. There was a wooden chair, a chest of drawers with a looking-glass and a small washstand, and there was not room for much more. She went to her window, drew the blind aside and peered out into the darkness. Omnibuses and cabs were driving hither and thither, and across the square she could see the long rows of lights in the ward windows, and dimly discern the outline of the hospital. She took off her hat and jacket and was searching for her key to open her trunk, when a knock came at the door and a nurse entered.

"Mrs. Faithful sent me to show you the way to your room. Nurse Constance, I suppose," she said, "and I may as well introduce myself as Nurse Burdett."

She had a pleasant face and gentle manners, and looked to Constance the very ideal of a nurse in her clean print dress and apron, and neat little mob cap.

"You are tired, I expect," she went on, noticing something much like tears on Constance's face. "Have you travelled far?"

Constance felt almost like choking as she replied, "From York. Yes, I am rather tired, but I shall be all right to-morrow."

She followed her companion through the long passage and down the flight of stone stairs into a small but pleasant-looking room. An elderly lady dressed in black and with snowy-white hair was seated at a writing-table. She got up as they entered, and telling Nurse Burdett she might leave them, greeted her new probationer.

Constance noticed at once that she had a stern face, though she looked kindly at her, and she thought she was as stately as a queen. She made her sit down and warm herself, whilst she asked her a few questions, and told her she should begin work next morning, but that she need not go to the hospital by seven as the others did, as she would take her across herself after the doctor's morning visit. She then rose and led the way across the hall to a large room from which the sound of voices intermingled with cups and saucers reached them.

THE "UNLUCKY" OPAL.

By EMMA BREWER.

" What radiant changes strike the astonished sight,
What glowing hues of mingled shade and light ! "—*Falconer.*

o the lover of the rare and beautiful who is untroubled by caprice or fashion there is no gem so dear as the opal with its flashes of brilliant hues. A writer, 500 B.C., said, "The delicate colour and tenderness of the opal reminds me of a loving and beautiful child ; " and Pliny described it well when he wrote, "The opal unites within itself the colours of the ruby, amethyst, and emerald, in the most marvellous mixture, and its fire is like the flame of burning sulphur." It has been considered by some that a gem so beautiful, delicate, and pure, ought to be of celestial origin ; but although this cannot be proved, it may with truth be affirmed that there is a deep mystery connected with the opal both in its composition and physical properties. That which gives value to this gem is its wonderful play of coloured reflections, which concentrates within it all the glories of the rainbow, and yet if the interior of the opal is examined there is nothing to account for it. Indeed, this precious stone has no colour that may be properly called its own, except a faint bluish tinge something like the tint of quartz, to which mineral it is evidently closely related. For proof of this, break an opal, when it will be seen that all its colours perish. The best conclusion arrived at is that the opal is full of nearly invisible fissures, and that water and air are the mysterious agents working in these tiny crevices in producing and perfecting the beautiful colours.

The opal, like the emerald, is formed of silica or sand, but without the aid of glucina and alumina—it is simply sand with the addition of ten to twelve per cent. of water.

In two or three points it differs from other precious stones. 1st. It cannot possibly be imitated. 2nd. It never crystallises in regular and definite form. 3rd. When it is first taken from the earth it is soft, but hardens and diminishes in bulk by exposure to the air.

The true beauties of the opal are only to be seen when it is moved about, then it appears to have an actual life within it. It is a very fragile stone and requires great skill and care in cutting. It has from time to time been engraved, but it is always a hazardous proceeding on account of the numberless fissures in the stone which it is dangerous to open in the air.

The precious or noble opal came formerly almost entirely from Hungary, and although it was taken hence to India to gain for it the name of Oriental, it has no home there. The matrix of the Hungarian opal is in a kind of felspar rock which yields also lead, silver and gold. The peculiarity of these special opals is that they show a uniform milkiness of surface more or less iridescent, and experience teaches that they resist the effects of wear longer than any other sort, and for this cause are the most valuable.

Opals are found also in Honduras in much the same condition as in Hungary.

During the last few years precious opals of great beauty have been found in Queensland in thin veins of brown ironstone, and bid fair to rival the famous Hungarian stones. "They are at present largely used for cameos, the brilliant colours of the gem forming a marked contrast to the dark background afforded by the ironstone matrix."

The opal has also been discovered in New South Wales in beds of sandstone. Fine stones of large size are rarely found anywhere, indeed they seldom exceed an inch in diameter, and are sold by the piece and not by the carat, if we except a few of the fine specimens of Hungary.

Mr. Streeter says "There is no doubt that the opal mass, originally in a liquid or gelatinous condition, filled up the cavities in the felspar veins and became gradually solidified."

There have been one or two black opals discovered in Egypt but these are very rare ; " they have the glow of the ruby seen through a mist like a coal ignited at one end." It is a curious fact that opals are much more brilliant on a hot day, and therefore a jeweller always holds one in his warm hand before showing it.

In ancient times and during the Middle Ages, indeed down to the time of Sir Walter Scott, the opal was believed to bestow on the wearer unmixed good. It was certainly the favourite gem of the Romans in their best periods of intelligence and refinement ; so far from being feared in these early times it was eagerly sought for, as it was supposed to possess the power of warning against disaster, and as being "the rosy herald of joy."

The beauty and charm of the opal may be imagined by the fact that at a time when banishment to a Roman was worse than death, one of the senators preferred this to parting with his gem.

This opal, the most famous in history, was the property of the Roman Senator Nonius, who wore it as a ring. Its size was scarcely larger than a hazel nut, but it was so beautiful and perfect that it was valued at the enormous sum of £125,000. Marc Antony desired earnestly to possess this opal in order to make it a present to Cleopatra Queen of Egypt, but Nonius refused to part with it, for it was the idol of his heart, and he sought safety in flight, content to be a beggar also for its sake. After many centuries of prosperity a time of adversity came to the opal. It was deprived of everything save its beauty, and instead of being the harbinger of good was looked upon with superstitious dread and as a gem to be avoided ; and this change of fortune is supposed to have been brought about by Sir Walter Scott, who had no love for jewels, and who introduced this among others in his *Anne of Geierstein*, and made it play so ignoble a part that henceforth no one cared to wear it for fear of its bringing ill-luck. He makes Anne of Geierstein say, "Of all the gauds which the females of my house have owned, this (the opal) perhaps has been the most fatal to its possessors." If a Russian of either sex or of any rank should happen to see an opal among goods submitted for purchase he or she will buy nothing that day, for the opal to a Russian is an embodiment of the evil eye.

Fortunately the good common-sense of our Queen in giving her daughters an opal ring as a marriage gift is gradually removing the ban imposed by Sir Walter Scott, and allowing us once again to enjoy its beauty without fear of direful consequences.

A very interesting story is told of the mysterious action of an opal by A. C. Hamlin. I quote it in full.

"A traveller," he says, "from Central America brought home a splendid rough fire opal which dazzled the eye with its fiery reflections. We took it to an honest lapidary, who received it with a doubtful look. The next day the opal was returned having been shaped into the usual oval form, but only a faint gleam of any of the coloured rays flashed from its surface or the interior. Is this the gem we gave you yesterday ? we demanded of the artisan. With a smile the lapidary took the transparent stone and roughened its finely polished surface upon the wooden wheel.* In an instant the lost fire returned as if directed by a magic wand The perfect transparency of the gem with its high polish had allowed the rays of light to pass directly through it, and there was but little refraction, but on the roughening of the surface the light was interrupted and the peculiar property of the mineral displayed. Unfortunately the lesson was not concluded here. At the last touch of the wheel the beautiful gem flew into two parts and its glories departed in an instant. Saddened with the day's experience we took the two fragments and cemented them together and tossed the stone into a drawer which contained other mineral specimens of no great value. Some months after while searching for a misplaced stone a gleam of light suddenly flashed out as we opened the drawer. It was the neglected and abused opal which now gleamed with the energy of a living coal of fire. It had recovered its beautiful reflections, and still adorns, notwithstanding its fracture, a most cherished jewel."

There have been one or two famous opals besides that of Nonius ; one was an exquisite harlequin opal belonging to the financier D'Anguy before the revolution of the last century. By harlequin is meant an opal with patches of colour of every hue.

The two largest precious opals known in this country were found in the Hungarian mines in 1866, and exhibited by the late Madame Goldschmidt in the Paris Exhibition of 1867. One weighed 186 carats and the other, a magnificent harlequin opal, 160 carats.

One of the finest known in modern times was that belonging to the Empress Josephine ; it was called The Burning of Troy, from the number of red flames blazing on its surface ; and there were some good specimens in the Hope Collection, one of which was an inch long and three quarters of an inch wide, whose reflected rays were green and yellow interspersed with flashes of bright blue and deep red. A representation of Apollo's head surrounded by rays of fire is engraved upon it in high relief. It is supposed to be very ancient and of Persian workmanship.

Another of value is an intaglio on a large opal of the portrait of Louis XIII. when he was a child.

---

* The opal is cut and polished first upon a leaden plate covered with emery, next on a wooden wheel with fine pumice stone, and lastly on a wheel covered with felt, so delicate is the handling necessary to turn out an opal to best advantage.

"I GAZED ACROSS THE SEA OF LIFE WITH YOUTHFUL EYES."

" I knew my life
.in me and expand, and all
which so nearly is divine
I." *

ere the evening chamber con-
.ed pupils, very bright and
ose brilliantly-lighted rooms
g people, with a sort of House
'rofessors and masters, and a

n the " Epic of Hades."

running current of pleasant chatting in the intervals between the pieces of the programme. Very refreshing too, that delightful pause for tea and conversation when favoured students were well taken care of. This child was happy enough to have Sterndale Bennett often as her chaperon (and how popular and charming be was, all who had the happiness of knowing him will agree), besides her other masters who looked after the tired and timid girl who felt so happy in their care. Even

now, so long after, the bright happy rooms full of excited young people (all save the few Dons were students), the hum of those young sweet voices, the (not unwelcome) clatter of tea and coffee cups, and the moving crowds with their very audible and decided opinions (young people are so decided in their infallible judgments) form a bright pageant of the past which is very real still to the grateful girl who was so happy then and met with such generous kindness.

(To be continued.)

AMERICAN SLANG, CATCH-WORDS AND ABBREVIATIONS.

By DORA DE BLAQUIÈRE.

ELL. as I knew the quaintness of the "slang," and, indeed, of the American colloquial language altogether (which perhaps should hardly be called "slang"), I never was quite so much struck by it as traversed the United States and ourney to the "Great Show," lbian Exhibition at Chicago. comical, and the fun is added-imes by the fact that no one that light; and the words or so common that they have iced.

th the old lady who travelled Niagara, and told me she a money, as well as her farm, t considerable to have to climb . back seat at her time of life." visit round for a spell," she .y daughter lives out west in ould admire to see you out en her a good home, and she's han, though she ain't home to wours her par, and he was as wrushwood fence." We bad her, mine ancient chum and I, quite a shine" to me, as she ine of her many confidences oad golden religion, and in all d been a waiter on Provi-last I heard of her was, 1e to "hustle" or I'd never "You have to hustle," she you forget it at the Bridge." ustle" indeed! but I thus successfully.

and in Canada, the word nost constant sound you hear, presses on you that "you'll whatever you are about to do. the tram-cars, and the train," ny chance, you have to meet ustle" more than ever. As ne, it is the most dreadful world.

:h on cake," exclaims a young ays everything is "just too : has "seen such a lovely also talks about a "brainy" rd being much applied in e and to things. A "brainy" s clever and able, in the tive. "You have a brick in get tipsy; and if this be not you reply, "It's not my t certainly is not, in the sense yet dead).

ike" and "bad hat," or, as say, "a bad egg," have both

made their bows before an English audience; and we also know the ugly and everlastingly-used word "boodle" and "boodler." This is really a Dutch word meaning, in its proper sense, "property left by a relation," a "testator." It always means money in its present sense; but not money honestly got. In contradistinction to "boodling," a man will assure you that the money is "straight money," i.e. honestly come by. Judging by the charges made in various newspapers, political money is always "boodled."

"He just tore past me like a streak of greased lightning. I guess that buggy won't be worth shucks when he stops," is a vivid description of a runaway of double-distilled swiftness. "Shucks" are the outer skins of the corn-cobs, and of course are quite valueless. If you have got on your "store clothes" you are what we should call a "swell," but if you are "going it" to an even greater extent, you are "cutting a big swathe," a term derived from the wielding of the scythe in hay-time.'

An "air line" means the most direct route. If you were in the backwoods you would say, you "went across lots," i.e. across the fields. "Slantendicularly" means to go crookedly, or on one side. "I can't get with her," is the method of saying that you don't get on with a person; and if some plan or attempt have been a failure, if you said, in the west, that it did not "pan out right," everyone would understand that the man who "bossed" the job had made a failure in some way, and matters had not turned out as was anticipated.

"As mad as mad," and "as savage as a meat axe," are both ordinary expressions. "Acted real mean" is another; and if you were abusive you would probably be exhorted to "dry up and not pile up the agony like that." It is a very funny habit also when you ask someone: "Is this yours?" to hear them say, "Well, it's not anyone else's;" and "don't you forget it," is the commonest addition to every piece of proffered information. "You didn't think I belonged to that crowd, did you?" was the scathing answer to an inquiry as to the invited guests at a picnic.

In Canada you hear much of the "Chore boy," and in the backwoods in May, when the black flies are bad, he weeds the garden "enveloped in the smoke of a smudge," the latter word meaning a smoke made by kindling a fire in an old tin pan with damp wood. A smudge is used to keep off mosquitoes; and I have seen half-a-dozen burning round a house on a summer evening, in the hope of affording a little rest from their torture.

In the north-western parts of Canada you drive about on a "buckboard," which is a machine having four wheels, a floor laid between them on the springs, and a seat in the centre—a dreadfully ramshackle affair.

But when you go over the country roads and find that your horse picks his way through rocks, and that your carriage is expected to go over them, you realise that nothing very solidly built could surmount such difficulties and such real dangers. But oh! the beauty of the woods in Canada in May, when the dogwood and the lilies are all in flower; the dog's-tooth-violets also, and the forget-me-nots blossom under-foot. Or, when in the hush of the early morning you waken in time to hear the great forest around you wakening up too, with the "drumming" of the partridge, or the prolonged cry of the whip-poor-wills, there is a peculiar enchantment in your surroundings.

Out on these northern lakes they catch fish by "trolling," and when a man says he "trolled home," you know he has hung a fishing-line from the stern of the boat, with a bit of tin to glitter and attract the fish. And it is in these "diggings" that, when you "go to see your best girl," the process called courtship becomes of a more electric nature, and is called "sparking." There, too, they take "store pay," which means that wages are paid in kind, by an order on the store for a certain amount. There also whiskey becomes "tangle-leg," a very good name too, for it does cause much confusion amongst men's legs sometimes; and you make acquaintance with the word "crank," a much-meaning term, and if they look out for their own interests, "they have an axe to grind." "Bass" is in universal use, and "the boss has been there, and knows all about it," and most likely you will find he is "the biggest toad in the swamp." The expression that most rejoiced me was "stay put." "I've put it up several times, and it won't stay put." What lots of things I have known in life that don't "stay put!"

The quaintness of the native American humour is at times wonderful. A very good instance of it was given the other day in a weekly paper, in the shape of a story about a distressed and deeply-mourning widow. A friend who is inquiring for her, says sympathetically, "Poor dear, I suppose she takes no comfort out of anything, not even music." "Oh, yes she does," was the answer, "she plays the piano, but on account of her mourning she only uses the black keys."

In an American paper I found the following collection of political proverbs, which I think are excellent, terse, sensible, and witty:—

"Thar's never a short crop ov polliticks."
"A statesman that stays pore, ought never to be out ov a job."
"'Honerable,' before some men's names don't kno what it is thar fer."
"A politishan that kin lie, and won't, is kep purty bizzy exercizin his ability."
"Some men that is in favor of paper money

will vote fer silver, and take thar pay in gold; and *visy versy*."

"Don't look a boughten vote in the mouth."

"An aingel in polliticks will shed its wings after the first campane."

The use of abbreviations in America is very extraordinary, especially on the railroads. A gentleman told me he had gone to the ticket-office—I think, in Chicago—and had asked what was the best route to St. Louis; the clerk said at once, "St. Louis? Go over the C. B. and G., C. R. I., and P. A. T., and S. F., C. and A. I. C. L., and S. W." This seems what would be called over there "as clear as mud;" but, after all, it is only the names of the railways you must traverse to get to your destination.

The negroes are amongst the most amusing of the people you meet, even on the cars. The porter (as he is called) of the "sleepers" gave me no end of amusement; and the following, which I hope you will enjoy, is a capital specimen of negro talk.

"I'm po'ly, honey, po'ly. Ky'ant spec' to hold togedder much longer, wid de pains roun' hyar, an' numony lyin' roun' in de chest, an' cramps constant. I'm breakin', breakin' fas'. De good Lord sen's punishment to dem dat needs His 'flictin' rod; He's gettin' me ready, I s'pose. But de debbil, he trabbels fas'; done catch up ef I doan be mighty spry."

As she went on the old woman swayed her body to and fro, repeating the tale of her misfortunes as if to an inward accompaniment of merriment. Her laugh seemed to have spread over the entire surface of her whole frame.

Then all at once a sudden seriousness seized upon her. She leaned over close to Glory to whisper with suppressed eagerness:

"Yer ain't done got married yet, chile?"

"No," Glory replied lightly, looking down in the earnest black face. She was laughing now into the solemn eyes fixed upon her.

"No, not yet, Sukey; nobody'll have me."

"How ole you gettin', chile?" The black eyes rebuked Glory's levity by a still more impressive solemnity in their gaze.

"I'm nineteen, Sukey, las' May."

"Fer goodness' sake, honey, done hurry up and kotch some un!" cried the negress, holding up her chocolate arms in the fervour and heat of her admonition. But Glory continued to smile, the smile broadening into a laugh at the old woman's tragic view of the hopelessness of her still unmated condition.

"The trouble is, Sukey, there isn't anybody to catch," Glory answered at last through her laugh.

"Dar mus' be some un, honey; de Lord nebber meant gals like you ter go fru life ole maids : 'tain't de way de Lord works, nohow. Dar's some un'll 'ong, you jes see ef dar woan. Hit look like dat to me; he's roun' de corner, un mebbe yer'll fine him knockin' at de do' when you get home. An' you jes le'h 'im in, honey; done mek no great ter-do, for dar aiu't no time ter lose, nohow. An', honey," continued the negress, with increasing fervour of intensity, as she took hold of Glory's falling skirts with both her strong black hands, and lifted her shining face, glistening with the warmth of her appeal, "you jes' be kyarful how you maries de second time. Fus' time ain't no account, nohow; dey's sure ter die or be killed off, or somethin' happens, likely 'nuff. But de second one, he's de one dat stays by yer—he's dar, sure's yer skin, an' dar ain't no gettin' rid ob him no more'n rheumatics or de taxes; he's roun' constant. You 'member what 'spectable nigger Jeff was, my fust husband? Well, Ben, you know, he's diff'rent; he's jes' a low-down, no 'count nigger, lyin' roun' drinkin' and cussin' 'nuff ter try de sper-rit ob der archangel. Goodness knows I'se had 'nuff ob second husbands."

The military term "baggage" does duty where we, in England, should use "luggage," and here we have not yet adopted the "All aboard," which is the universal signal for the starting off of every form of conveyance, from a "buggy" to a tramcar or railway train. Nor have we either the term "deadhead" for the person who holds a free pass; nor yet adopted the phrase "He's a rustler," though, iu its place, we do say, "He's a daisy," meaning much the same thing.

When the true American inquires "Where are my gums?" you need not think she is alluding in any way to her mouth; she only means to inquire for her goloshes; and should she ask your "given name" you will know she means what we should call the Christian name and not the surname. The funniest misnomer which one hears is in the northern parts of Canada, where people talk about "lunch;" if you chance to arrive in the middle of the night, the meat you would partake of would be called "lunch," and if you started with an early breakfast, that would be "lunch," too. In fact, I found that all meals eaten out of due season were "lunches," and the real lunch has no existence where there is perpetually early dinner.

And now I think I have almost come to the end of my notes, save one, which I must chronicle. Upon one of the northern lakes of Canada someone in my bearing asked, "What So-and-so was doing now?" (meaning, of course, whether he had any employment). The answer of his brother was at once funny and spoke a volume as well. "Oh, he ain't doing much, he mostly takes it out looking round," and I will end with the Western and Southern form of salutation and adieu—

"So-long, So-long!"

PRECIOUS STONES; THEIR HOMES, HISTORIES, AND INFLUENCE.

THE TURQUOISE, AND CAT'S EYE.

By EMMA BREWER.

THE TURQUOISE.

A clear sky, free from all clouds, will most excellently discover the beauty of a true turquoise.—*Thos. Nicols.*

HE turquoise, which is an emblem of prosperity, has, by reason of its beauty and mysterious gifts, attained to the high rank of a precious stone.

It is now, as it has ever been, a general favourite, although it is neither transparent nor does it occur in crystals.

Old writers delight to tell of its power and influence for good, and its detestation of vice, and were never tired of declaring that it was one of God's wonderful gifts to man bestowed upon him for his use and contemplation in order that he might be strengthened in grace and virtue and in the avoidance of evil.

The sympathy of the turquoise with its owner has been rich in suggestions for poets—

"And true as turkois in the dear lord's ring
Look well or ill with him."*

Again,

"As a compassionate turkois that doth tell,
By looking pale, the wearer is not well."

The turquoise was believed to protect its wearer by taking upon itself any danger that threatened, but in order to receive all the advantages which this stone was supposed to grant the wearer must have received it as a gift and not by purchase. It is a proverb in Russia that a turquoise given by a loving hand carries with it happiness and good fortune. And another, "that the colour of a turquoise pales when the well-being of the giver is in peril," and the modern superstition is that "the turquoise is a sovereign defence against mortal wounds."

The historian, Boetius de Boot, relates the following as coming within his own experience, and shows his firm belief in the mysterious properties of the turquoise.

"The turquoise had been thirty years in the possession of a Spaniard who resided within a short distance of my father's house. Upon his death, his furniture and effects were exposed for sale, as is the custom with us. Among other articles was this turquoise ring; but al-though many persons, admirers of its extraordinary beauty during its late master's lifetime, were now come to buy it, no one would offer for it, so entirely bad it lost its colour. In fact it was more like a malachite than a turquoise. My father and brother, who had also gone with the intention of purchasing it, being well acquainted with its perfections, were amazed with the change. My father bought it notwithstanding, being induced to do so by the low price put upon it. On his return home, however, ashamed to wear so mean-looking a gem, he gave it to me, saying, 'Son, as the virtues of the turkois are said to exist only when the stone has been given, I will try its efficacy by bestowing it upon thee.' Little appreciating the gift, I had my arms engraved upon it as though it had been an agate or other less precious stone such as are used for seals and not for ornaments. I had not worn it a month before it resumed its pristine beauty and daily seemed to increase in splendour.' This, however, was not all. De Boot still further relates that he was travelling home to Bohemia from Padua, where he had been to take his doctor's degree, when in the dark his horse stumbled and fell with his rider from a bank on to the road ten feet below. Neither horse nor rider were the worse, but when he washed his hands on the following morning he perceived that the turquoise was split in two. He had the larger portion reset and continued to wear it, when again he met with an accident

* Ben Jonson.

which was like to have caused him a broken limb, and again the turquoise took the fracture upon itself and had to be reset.

The turquoise has always been a favourite gem for the betrothal ring, notwithstanding that the beauty of its colour is said to depend upon the constancy of its giver, and therefore must often be productive of pain to the wearer.

That it is still in favour as a wedding-gift we see by the present offered by the people of Kensington to Miss Borthwick on her marriage with Earl Bathurst, consisting of a turquoise bracelet and brooch.*

A couple of centuries ago a man scarcely thought himself dressed unless he wore on his finger a turquoise ring.

Queen Elizabeth always wore a turquoise ring, by whom given is not recorded. At her death it was taken from her finger by a lady in waiting and thrown out of the window to Sir John Harrington, who hurried with it to James VI. of Scotland as a sign of the death of the queen.

Another ring with a history is the turquoise of Shylock stolen by his daughter.

Although this gem was so highly prized in the Middle Ages it does not appear to have been known to the ancients, for among the numerous precious stones furnished by Persia and noted in the literary remains of antiquity the turquoise has no place.

At the present time, however, the gem *par excellence* of Persia is the turquoise, and a very interesting account of its mines and miners has been drawn up by Mr. Schindler, the recent director of the mines, and forwarded to our Foreign Office.

The celebrated turquoise mines, evidently those mentioned by Tavernier as three days journey from Meshed, and furnishing the most beautiful old rock turquoise, are situate in a district which Mr. Schindler calls Maden, about forty square miles in extent within the province of Nishapur, Khorassin. The villages of the district contain a population of about 1200, who are almost entirely occupied with the obtaining, cutting, and selling of turquoises.

The turquoise veins run between porphyry, limestone, and sandstone, never higher than 5800 feet above the level of the sea, nor lower than 4800. The climate is excellent; wheat, barley, and mulberry trees grow well at a height of 5000 feet, and fig-trees on the slopes 6000 feet above the level of the sea.

Nearly all the men engaged in the turquoise industry are inveterate opium smokers, and many of the women have also acquired the vice. The gain of turquoises has made the people careless of all else, and yet there are very few of the inhabitants who possess anything worth speaking of, in fact they live from hand to mouth like most people whose income is uncertain. A good turquoise is found, and the money obtained by its sale is spent at once. It is no unusual thing at the mines to see men who pay yearly to the Government a tax of sixty tomans,† that is about £20, and who beyond this gain one hundred and fifty tomans, £50, having literally nothing to eat.

The turquoise mines are of two kinds: first, the mines proper having shafts and galleries in the rocks, and secondly, the kháki mines or diggings, in the detritus of disintegrated rock washed down towards the plain.

The treasures of the former are difficult to arrive at, seeing that they are partly filled by rubbish and are often unsafe to work in. It is only during the last thirty or forty years that blasting with gunpowder has been resorted to by the miners; formerly all the work was done by picks, and much better, for they extracted the turquoises entire, while the

gunpowder, doing more work, often breaks the stones into small pieces.

The kháki or diggings extend from the foot of the mountain a mile or two into the plain, and here in alluvial soil some of the best stones are found. Work is carried on without any system; the earth is brought to the surface, sifted and searched, the latter being done by children. The fine turquoise presented to the Shah, valued at £2000, as well as many other very fine ones, have been found in the diggings or kháki. Still the work here is more of the character of a speculation than in the mines proper.

The findings are divided into three classes, the very best are called "ring-stones," and sold by the piece. The colour of these must be fast and of the deep blue of the sky; a small speck of a lighter shade or an almost inappreciable tinge of green decreases the value considerably. There is also that indefinable property of a good turquoise called the "zát," something like the "water" of a diamond and the "lustre" of a pearl, and even a fine-coloured turquoise without the "zát" is of very little worth.

The second best are called "bárkháneh" turquoises, and are sold by the pound at the mines for about £90 per pound for the best, and about £25 per pound for the lowest or fourth quality.

Only the best of these second stones find their way into the European market, and although some are used by jewellers for rings, the fact that the miners do not class them or sell them as "ring-stones" proves that they are not of the first quality. One can buy small cut turquoises of third quality in Persia at the rate of two or three shillings a thousand. These "bárkháneh" stones are frequently used by Persians for daggers, sword-hilts, and sheaths. Sir Richard Burton in his *Gold Mines of Midian* mentions having seen a bright blue turquoise set in the stock of a Bedouin matchlock, which had been exposed to wear and weather for fifty years, but had lost nothing of its colour.

Then there is the third class of findings called "Arabi" turquoises, a term used by the Persians for bad and unsaleable stones. Some of the miners when on a pilgrimage to Mekka had taken with them a quantity of bad turquoises, and had sold them well to the Arabs, hence they are called "Arabi."

Work in the mines proper is difficult owing to the unsafe condition of the galleries; but a miner rarely returns empty-handed, whereas at the diggings the work is comparatively easy, but the finding of turquoises is a matter of chance. It often happens that a miner after working hard for a few months in the mines, and having saved a few tomans, gets a fever fit on him to try his luck at the diggings, and he works till his savings have vanished and his tools pawned and nothing of worth to show for it, and then he goes back to the mines. The majority of good workmen rarely work out of the mines, but send their children to the diggings—there being no danger in the work there and maybe a chance of luck—and a sight of the people at the diggings will show you the young, the very old, the weak and the idle. During the summer months strangers come to Máhden to try their luck at the diggings.

The original finders of the turquoise do not gain much. The elders generally buy the stones direct from the workmen, and then sell them to merchants at Meshed or to agents who visit the mines. The first profit on turquoises is never less than ten per cent., and is often twenty per cent.; for example, one of the elders buys turquoises for ten tomans (that is ten times six shillings and eightpence) from the miners and sells them to an agent or middleman for twelve tomans, the agent sells them to the dealers in Meshed for four-

teen or fifteen tomans. The dealer sorts them and sells some in the country, and the remainder he sends to Moscow, where they are bought by special agents for European dealers. It is a safe calculation that turquoises bought of the miners for ten tomans are sold for twenty-five tomans in Europe. Mr. Schindler says it is strange that up to now European dealers have not thought it worth their while to send their own agents to the mines.

The miners rarely cut their own findings, and therefore do not often know the quality of the stones.

Enormous profits are often made on "ring-stones;" for example, a turquoise valued at Meshed at £300 was bought for £3 from the finder by an elder; he sold it uncut in Meshed for £38. After being cut it was sent to Paris, where it was valued at £600. The second purchaser only received £340 for it, the difference was gained by the agents.

The annual output of the mines proper and the diggings averaged for the last few years over £8300 value at the mines: the final purchasers probably pay three times this amount.

The turquoise in Persia is now as a rule cut by wheels made of a composition of emery and gum, whereas formerly it was cut on slabs of sandstone. The polishing is done generally by children on a slab of very fine grained sandstone.

The discovery of the true turquoise in Victoria, described by the Melbourne *Argus* a month or two since, and copied in the *Times* of Oct. 18, 1893, is looked upon as a phase of mining industry in that colony likely to be rich in results.

The pioneer, a man named Gascoigne, was a member of the Victorian mounted police force, whose hobby was collecting specimens of minerals from the various districts he visited. He was placed in the King River district, and while there made the acquaintance of a young man, a thorough bushranger. Asking him if he had ever come across gold in the district, he answered "No;" but that twelve miles away over the hills he had noticed veins of blue stone in the rocks, and nobody seemed to know what it was; the two men went off together, the bushman leaving the other to his search while he went further on to look for wild horses. Gascoigne, after a search, at length came across some grey, slaty rock in which there was a blue vein. With his clasp-knife he took out a number of pieces of the blue stone and submitted them to the School of Mines, and the secretary reported they were of little or no value.

Gascoigne was not satisfied with this, and on visiting Melbourne later he had the stone thoroughly tested by an Italian expert, who found it to be the true turquoise, a judgment which has since been thoroughly confirmed. Mining leases have been taken up, and everything is prospering, and it is believed that ere long turquoises from Australia will be competing in European markets with those that have been found for centuries in the famous mines of the Persian province of Khorassin.

One noteworthy feature about turquoise mining is, that although veins may be traced on or near the surface, the stone so found is generally affected by the surface-drainage and the atmospheric influences of countless centuries. Experience proves that the deeper down the miner goes, the better is his chance of finding stones of first-rate quality.

There are turquoise mines in Mount Sinai, the stones being here embedded in a matrix very much like that in which diamonds are found in Brazil. One of the hieroglyphic inscriptions in Sinai mentions the "Goddess Hathor, mistress of the land of the turquoises."

We have had some very good turquoises from Mexico. Among the ancient Mexicans it was a favourite material for inlaid mosaic work, of which some beautiful specimens may be seen in the British Museum.

The turquoise is the gem most frequently employed for amulets by the Orientals, who engrave sentences of the Koran upon it, filling in the characters with gold.

In 1808 a magnificent necklace of turquoise, consisting of twelve stones, was in the market; each stone was engraved in relief with a figure of one of the Cæsars.

The chemical nature of the turquoise has hitherto remained problematic as the results of investigations have never agreed; the only elements invariably present were alumina and copper. Mr. Streeter, however, gives its chemical composition thus—

Phosphorous pentoxide	32·8
Alumina	40·2
Water	19·2
Copper oxide	5·3
Iron and manganese oxides	2·5
	100·0

The turquoise, like all other precious stones, has its double. In this case it is the occidental turquoise, which is in fact a fossil ivory produced from the teeth of a past race of animals brought into contact with substances containing copper and iron. It differs entirely from the Oriental or old rock turquoise both in structure and in composition. It is also softer and more opaque than the true gem, and in some Eastern lands is preferred to the Oriental.

THE CAT'S EYE

stands next to the diamond and sapphire in hardness, and notwithstanding its name is a very beautiful gem, and one that has always been held in high esteem in India, where it is venerated as a charm against witchcraft; and in Ceylon, which is its special home, a native would rather part with anything in his possession than give up his cat's-eye, if he be lucky enough to have one.

The cat's-eye, which is a rare variety of chrysoberyl, is found in the form of rolled pebbles in the river-sands of Ceylon in company with sapphires, topaz, and other gems. Twin crystals of great beauty have been also found in the emerald mines of the Ural.

Its chief characteristic is a remarkable play of light running from end to end, the result, no doubt, of its internal structure, which seems to be full of minute channels. No matter what colour the ground-work may be, the line of light is nearly always white, and more or less iridescent, and it is upon the beauty, perfection, and number of these lines, which run across the middle of the stone, that the value of the gem is based.

The stone is of various colours from pale straw through all shades of brown, and from very pale apple green to the deepest olive. As the gem is moved about, it is beautiful with its soft deep colour, and its mysterious, luminous streak shifting restlessly from side to side, especially under a bright sunlight or gaslight.

It is not difficult to conceive an imaginative and superstitious people regarding this precious stone with awe; and, believing it to be the abode of spirits, they hold it sacred, fit only to dedicate to their gods.

There are three stones which bear a resemblance to the Oriental cat's-eye, but they will not bear the test of close comparison. The one which approaches most nearly is a variety of quartz called quartz cat's-eye, and it ought not to be possible for even the unlearned in precious stones to mistake this for the true; for example, the ray of light in the real is iridescent, in the false dull; the hardness in the real is 8·5, in the false 7; the specific gravity of the real is 3·8, of the false 2·6. The real cat's-eye often shows a beautiful dichroism, the false never. The composition also differs; in the true gem we find 80 parts alumina, 20 glucina, and for colouring matter oxide of iron: in the false 48 parts are silicon and 51 oxygen, with a small amount of oxide of iron and lime.

The difference between the two is also great in intrinsic worth, the one of great value, the other of little; the one used for personal ornaments, while the other is made into snuff-boxes or to form a thin veneer to small tables.

THE WARDS OF ST. MARGARET'S.

By SISTER JOAN.

CHAPTER XV.

A FRESH MOVE.

"All things come round to him who will but wait."—*Longfellow.*

IT was a bright spring morning in May; the trees were already showing signs of green, and the fresh youth and beauty all around sent forth a feeling of gladness into many hearts. Not only the absence of traffic in the London streets, but the very stillness in the air betokened it to be a Sunday, even before the church bells called to mind the fact, or the church-goers were to be seen, passing this way and that to their various places of worship.

Constance was walking quickly along a broad thoroughfare leading to one of the great squares. As she got nearer she saw a figure whom she recognised at once to be Mr. Seaton leaning against the low wall which protected the centre of the square. Instinctively she slackened her pace. He was evidently waiting for some one, for he kept looking about expectantly, and when he caught sight of Constance went forward to meet her. She noticed how pale and worn he looked as he held out his hand, and her heart smote her at once for having allowed herself to make such an appointment, and wondered what her people at home would think if they knew. She felt shy and awkward, and tried to throw it off by talking in a very unconcerned way about anything that came uppermost in her mind.

About a fortnight after the Christmas festivities Constance had received a letter from Mr. Seaton, asking her to marry him, and begging at least for some hope, if only in the far distance.

She had replied, hardly knowing indeed what she had said, except that she had refused him, and nothing further had passed between them, until a day or two previously, when he had again written, saying that he was up in town and was anxious for an interview, and as he did not wish to come to the hospital where he was so well known, suggested their meeting outside. Constance had no intention of accepting him when she made the appointment; she had always thought of him in connection with Nurse Rose, and could not realise that he was indeed in love with her.

The very fact of her apparent indifference made it difficult for Mr. Seaton to say what he had meant to, and Constance gave him no help. He had told her in his letter that he loved her, but now he appeared self-absorbed and awkward.

They wandered on into the parks without much thought of whither they were going, until Constance suddenly felt as if she must somehow put an end to it all, and suggested their going to church. Mr. Seaton reluctantly agreed, and they went into the first they came to. Neither, however, were in the mood for a service, and the one here jarred upon rather than harmonised with their feelings; both were relieved when it was over.

As they retraced their steps Mr. Seaton made a great effort, and told Constance something of what he wanted her to know. She listened, but still without comprehending how deep was his affection for her. She felt distressed and blamed herself for coming, but gave him the same answer she had done before.

"It is useless," he said somewhat sorrowfully but coldly, "to prolong our walk. We may as well say good-bye at once. I ought to have understood before that when you said 'No' you meant it."

Constance held out her hand. She wanted to make some apology, to say how sorry she was to have pained him; how much she really liked him (for she owned to herself she did like him very much), but how she had never thought of love until she had received his letter. This and much more she longed to say, but speech failed her. After a moment's silence she merely said good-bye, and said it so quietly and calmly that Mr. Seaton, as he walked back alone, was inclined to wonder if she possessed a heart at all.

Constance felt utterly wretched as she climbed the stairs to her room. "If she could only tell some one," she thought. She felt very much tempted to confide in Sister Adelaide, and ask her advice. She little guessed what warm sympathy she would have received had she done so, or how lovingly Sister Adelaide would have tried to help her.

One of the sisters meeting her on her way upstairs remarked as she passed, "How cold and tired you look, Sister Hamilton; church does not seem to have agreed with you this morning! I'm quite glad I stayed at home."

"No, I certainly will not tell anyone," Constance mentally remarked to herself. "It is quite sufficient that the thing has happened. I wish I could just sit down and think quietly instead of going straight back to my ward."

It was just as well she could not, and that she was kept very busy all the rest of that day and for some weeks to come, so much so that she had no time to think of herself, and required all her energies to get through each day's work as it came. Doctor Bell once mentioned to her that his nephew had thoughts of going abroad, as he did not care to start a practice on his own account.

He had never been able to find out whether there was anything between Mr. Seaton and Constance, and yet he had his suspicions that she was in some way connected with his unsettlement and the desire he had for change of scene and life.

Constance was busy at the time doing a dressing with a new house-surgeon, and though Doctor Bell looked anxiously for some show of feeling or surprise, she merely remarked without looking up: "I expect he will enjoy that

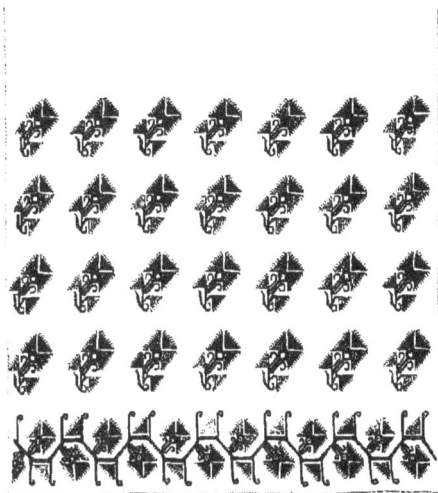

FIG. 2.—FINE EMBROIDERY FROM RHODES.

were made that were surrounded and protected from fraying, and these open spaces were so arranged that they left flat pieces of material as thick designs, and themselves formed the lighter parts of the design or the open grounding on which the heavy pattern rested. This peculiarity is seen in Lefka work. In many parts of it the old Greek lace designs are accurately reproduced, but in others the thick white embroidery with cotton, and the button-hole and satin-stitches more associated with embroidery than lace work appears. The designs are not very varied; they have evidently been blindly copied by mother and daughter for many generations, and no thought of change has penetrated to this Eastern nation, which, like all Oriental nations, abhors activity for mind or body. The only difference in the work is its fineness or coarseness, some villages working it upon very fine cotton foundations, others upon thick cottons. It is sold in long lengths, and is about half a yard in width of needlework, and it forms splendid sideboard cloths, bed-hangings, quilts, chair-backs, and sofa-backs. The fringe which forms the invariable finish is made from the unravelled threads knotted with tiny knots for a considerable length, and then allowed to hang down as left off with rather larger knots made as at the extreme end. Being all executed with white cotton the work washes and wears for many years.   B. C. SAWARD.

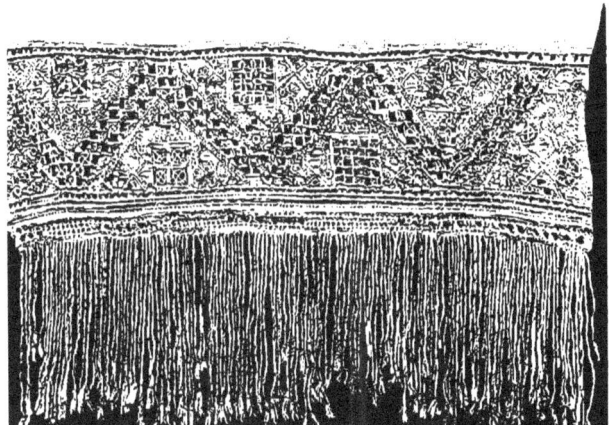

FIG. 3.—LEFKRA OR CYPRUS WORK.

PRECIOUS STONES; THEIR HOMES, HISTORIES, AND INFLUENCE.

By EMMA BREWER.

SEMI-PRECIOUS STONES.

CHRYSOPRASE, AMETHYST, GARNET, AMBER, AND CORAL.

stones yet to be spoken of, though classed as semi-precious, occupy places scarcely inferior to the precious, and are certainly equal to them in honour and interest. Chief among these are the stones mentioned at the head of this chapter.

The chrysoprase is of a beautiful apple-green colour, nearly transparent,[*] and capable of high polish. It is a green variety of chalcedony, and is generally found in company with the opal and other varieties of chalcedony and quartz.

It seems to have been known and used far back in the past, but it is only within the last hundred years that it has been traced to its true home and companions.

Its position in the walls of the new Jerusalem, Rev. xx., gives it a sacred and honourable distinction; and as far back as King Solomon's reign the chrysoprase was highly valued as one of the most fortunate of stones.

All through the reigns of the Georges, and up to about forty years ago, it was very fashionable for brooches and necklaces. These last were as a rule composed of nine oval half-slabs of chrysoprase, in form like the half of a small hen's egg, mounted with diamonds. One of the last made was by Mr. Streeter for the late Mrs. Henry Hope, of Piccadilly and Betchworth, and cost £1000.

Soon after this, chrysoprase completely fell out of fashion, and became a thing forgotten by the public; for, as the chrysoprase ornaments fell into the hands of firms like Rundell and Bridge, of Ludgate Hill, they were unmounted and thrown unceremoniously into a drawer as useless, and Hunt and Roskell, who were the successors of this firm, treated the chrysoprase ornaments in the same manner.

As a result the accumulation steadily increased, and on the retirement of Hunt and Roskell all these unmounted and broken pieces of chrysoprase were put up to auction and bought in by Mr. Streeter, who had them reduced to small pieces and cut *en cabochon*, and mounted in the most exquisite manner. The consequence was that the public taste was taken captive, and the stone so long despised and forgotten is now to be seen in the foremost ranks of fashionable life.

The Empress Frederick, who has been greatly interested in the reproduction of this stone, sent a quantity of it to Mr. Streeter from a mine on one of her estates, which he bought of her.

Many of the present generation look upon this stone as a new production of nature, while in reality it is but a long-forgotten beauty awaking from sleep with increased charms to attract and delight all who look

[*] When quite transparent you may be sure it is an imitation.

upon it; and it is not likely that it will ever again be subject to contempt and forgetfulness.

Beside being pleasant for the eye to look upon, it is believed to possess the power of bestowing certain blessings on the owner, such as assiduity in good works, gladness of heart, and an utter absence of covetousness.

It is no wonder, therefore, that at present the supply is not equal to the demand, which accounts for the number of imitations offered for sale, and which consist principally of dyed agate. The beautiful apple-green tints of the true chrysoprase are derived from oxide of nickel, which with a little water forms 2·5 of its composition; the 97·5 being silica.

Its real home is in Silesia, where it lives in the society of its friends and relations, the opal, chalcedony, and quartz.

THE AMETHYST.

" Last in the Holy City set,
With hues of glorious violet,
Forth from the amethyst are rolled
Sparks crimson bright and flames of gold;
The humble heart it signifies
That with its dying Master dies."

The word amethyst is supposed to be derived from the Greek verb to *intoxicate*, probably because of the belief that this stone was an antidote to drink and a charm against intoxication; indeed the ancients went so far as to say that wine, however strong, drunk from an amethyst cup, was incapable of producing intoxication.

It receives other names, according to the places where it is found. Its composition is very much like that of the chrysoprase, viz., silica, but with a different colouring matter, viz., oxide of magnesia, which gives it the beautiful violet tint.

It is dichroic, like the emerald; the one distinct tint being reddish-purple, and the other a bluish-purple. As an instance of its former value and subsequent fall, we would mention that Queen Charlotte had an amethyst necklace valued at £2000, which, apart from its historical associations, would not realise to-day more than £100.[*]

A very good amethyst was formerly equal to an Oriental diamond of its own size.

It was one of the stones of the breastplate of judgment, Ex. xxviii., and had its position in the walls of the New Jerusalem, Rev. xxi. It is emblematic of earthly sorrow, deep love, and faithfulness unto death.

The very best, called Oriental amethyst, is found in Brazil, Uruguay and Siberia, while the less rare may be found in many parts of the world.

Turkish women have always been fond of adorning themselves with it. As a rule the stones are polished in Venice and brought to Constantinople.

The composition of the amethyst is, as I have said, silica coloured by oxide of magnesia. Its hardness is the same as that of the chrysoprase, viz. 7.

THE GARNET.

The group of minerals known as garnet is extremely interesting to all who love precious and semi-precious stones. It has characteristics peculiarly its own, one of which is that it admits into its circle stones varying in

[*] Mr. Streeter.

colour, chemical composition, and eve specific gravity, insisting only upon crystallisation and the unchangeablene their fundamental form.

Variety of colour is, as I have notice hindrance to their admission into the c for garnets are red, orange red, green, a l tiful yellow or no colour at all, the to colouring being the amount of iron mo less which they have taken to themselve "iron is the great colourist of nature." [*]

The garnet that most of us know best a beautiful red colour which approaches nearly to that of the ruby, for which garn not infrequently mistaken, as you will seen in the chapter on rubies. It ough to be possible to make this error becau the difference in the hardness of the twe one being 9, the other only 7.

It probably derives its name from its e being like that of the blossom and kern the pomegranate, or it may be "granium," a grain, because it is so found in granular form.

The surroundings of its home depend much upon the part of the world in whic home is situate; it suits itself to circumst as we should say. In Austria the crysta found in serpentine, in the Zillerthal in cb slate, in Sweden in micaschist. In the Sir Pass between Brieg and Domo d'Ossola are discovered in the glacier streams, and i United States they are found in granite, in Brazil their companions are diamonds a rule they are found in alluvial soils in the of pebbles, grains, or masses. Very garnets come from the Ural, and the Bohemia are quite famous; you may see beautifully mounted in the jewellers' sho Dresden, Prague, and Vienna.

The most beautiful is the Oriental or garnet, so called from the river Siria in and not from the country Syria; and the some lovely ones found in Ceylon and E nearly if not quite equal to these in b and value.

There are eight kinds of garnet, f which only are used for jewellery. It was more valuable in early days, being equal diamond of its own size. The Pegu gar the only one at present which comma high price.

Quite lately some lovely garnets have found in Central South Australia; the called Australian rubies, and it has difficult even for experts to decide wh they are rubies or garnets.

New varieties of garnet have lately into our market from Siberia; they are brilliant, of a beautiful green colour an like any stones we know of.

AMBER.

The Eastern fictions about preciou semi-precious stones, as we know, mitted through many ages, and wer delight of old writers, and often, as i case of amber, prevented any desire to the true nature of the stone.

An imaginative abbot, for example, opinion that amber was honey melted l sun, dropped into the sea from the mou and congealed by water; while Nicia historian asserts that "the heat of th is so intense in some regions that it o the earth to perspire and the drops, c lating, form the substance called ambe

[*] Haüy.

ese drops of perspiration are carried ꞏea into Germany."

e is a couplet of the fireworshippers gives a still stranger origin, and is as

—

ınd thee shall glisten the loveliest ımber,
ever the sorrowing sea-bird hath wept."

rding to some poets, the sisters of ı, who were changed into poplar-trees banks of the Po, wept tears of amber ia'ly for their brother, who was slain tning.

Greeks held the following graceful n :—"The juices distilling from new ıd solidified by the sun are received by ning river, and borne as offerings to des of Italy;" while the Gauls ac-ꞏl for amber as being the divine drops l from the eyes of Apollo at the death on Æsculapius.

er has been known from the earliest ınd a philosopher who lived 600 years oke of its property of attracting light such as chaff and straw, in the same ıt the loadstone attracts iron; and it ꞏ than probable that this simple ob-ın was the foundation of the modern of electricity. Certainly, it is from the ıame *electron* that we derive our modern ꞏctric.

ꞏoubt the regard of the ancients for ꞏas maintained by the fabulous tales of ın and the mystery connected with it. ꞏarliest history of amber is to be found *Odyssey* of Homer,* where, in the list of ꞏffered by the Phœnician traders to the of Syria, stands a gold necklace hung ꞏs of amber. In such repute was it in in the time of Pliny that he sarcasti-marks that the price of a small figure er, however minute, exceeds that of a ꞏealthy slave. In his time, too, it was ꞏlieved that a collar of amber, worn he neck of a child, was a preservation secret poison and a counter-charm witchcraft and sorceries, and it has ꞏe fashion through many generations ꞏng children to wear necklaces of these indeed, it is only during the last fifty has fallen into disuse.

ꞏng precious substances employed as ꞏnts, the yellow amber played a grand ꞏarly times, and the efforts made to it were largely instrumental in carry-ꞏ germs of civilisation into countries ꞏp to that time had remained outside ꞏure of the world.

ꞏout the commerce of amber the an-ꞏavigators, especially the Phœnicians, never have heard mention of the ꞏn Seas, where this substance has its During the reign of Nero an expedi-ıs sent from Rome to explore the producing country (the Baltic coasts), ꞏ successful was it that it brought ꞏ a present to the emperor 13,000 lbs.

yellow amber, which is transparent, ꞏtly envelops insects,† plants, and ꞏ showing that it formerly was in a ꞏtate, and that the process of solidifying w.

er, notwithstanding all the mystery has surrounded it, is in reality only a ꞏesin, composed of carbon, hydrogen, ꞏ a little clay, alumina, and silica, the ıt forming 88¾ parts out of the 100. ın heated, it gives off certain organic and leaves a black residue, which is

---

used in the manufacture of the finest black varnishes.

The amber most esteemed is transparent and of a beautiful lemon colour. It is much valued in the East for mouthpieces for pipes and cigars because of the belief that amber never allows the transmission of any infection.

It is found mostly in the great plains of Germany and along the coast of the Baltic in a loose clayey sandstone called blue earth, while occasionally it occurs in beds of bitu-minous wood. The amber-gatherers have two or three methods of collecting it ; they dig it from the soil, pick it from the cliffs or collect the pieces cast on the shore by the waves ; these last are probably washed out of strata of brown coal by the action of the water.

In last year's report it was stated by the British Consul at Dantzic that the supply of amber is now limited to the out-put of the mine in East Prussia and is practically a monopoly, and that the small quantities found in other places scarcely pay the working expenses. In 1892 about sixty tons of raw amber arrived in Dantzic to be worked into beads and ornaments which find a sale in the East of Europe and in some parts of Africa.

The new process of pressing the small pieces of amber together and thus utilising what was formerly only melted down for varnish has disturbed the market, and amber is not so much sought after as formerly.

A short time since we went over a large factory in Austria in order to see the working up of amber into pipes and cigar-holders. We saw the rough pieces of yellow amber which had come from the North Sea, and the black amber or *schall* as it is called, which to our surprise we heard came from England. The first thing the work-people did was to cut off what is termed the shell, a certain amount of which is found on all amber, and then it is worked on the lathe by steel instru-ments, and polished on a leaden wheel with pumicestone and water. We noticed how much clearer and brighter some of the amber was than other, and were told that it depended greatly on the quality which varied very much. About a hundred gross of amber pipes are made in this one factory every week, beside innumerable cigar-holders. A good deal of amber is from time to time picked up on our own East coast.

CORAL.

"We wandered where the dreamy plain
Murmured above the sleeping wave :
And through the waters clear and calm
Looked down into the coral cave."
                              J. C. P.

"Heo is coral for goodnesse"
        Harleian MS., about 1200 A.D.

"The coral which wards off the thunderbolt and preserves from violent death."
                              14*th Cent.*

There are many varieties of coral ; but we have only to speak of that called precious, which is composed of carbonate of lime and animal secretion. It is the production of gelatinous creatures called polypi, whose dwell-ing is almost entirely in the tropics. They are extremely like the sea anemone, the one great difference being that they have the power of secreting a dense calcareous skeleton out of the lime found abundantly in every sea. It seems almost miraculous that such great works should be performed by such tiny creatures.

The precious coral is like a tree with leafless branches, about a foot high and an inch thick, though on rare occasions it is as thick as a man's body. These branches require about twelve years to attain the length of ten or twelve

---

inches, and the thickness necessary to cut them into beads for necklaces and ornaments, and so great is the care taken while fishing for coral that the same ground is never gone over twice in that period.

The mode of obtaining the coral is by drawing among the rocks a heavy cross of wood weighted with stones, and its edges covered with twisted hemp of coarse netting, and the wood as it rubs along the under sur-face of the rocks breaks off the coral branches, which get entangled in the netting and are thus drawn to the surface. Coral reefs are in reality beds of limestone ; the largest existing coral structure is the great Barrier Reef of Australia.

It is as difficult for us to describe the coral-building animal as it was for Punch's railway porter to describe an old lady's tortoise. He declared, "that being neither a dawg nor a bird, it must needs be a hinsec' ! "

Until the 18th century it was believed that coral was a tree living and developing itself under the sea. It was a Frenchman in 1727 who established its real nature, and showed that the flowers of this tree were radiated animals and that the coral was gradually formed by them. There are few objects which show more clearly than coral the power of Nature to effect her designs by feeble objects, and it requires an intimate knowledge of the habits of the coral-building creatures to credit what stupendous submarine reefs and islands are indebted for their structure to these tiny architects.

Coral is of various colours, but the red is by far the best and commands the highest price. The ancient Greeks called it " korallion," from two Greek words signifying " ornament " and " sea."

Orpheus, the poet of the Greeks, attributed wonderful powers to the coral, the gift of Minerva ; it baffled witchcraft, counteracted poison, protected from tempests and robbers, and, mixed in powder with seed-corn, secured growing crops from thunderstorms, blight, caterpillars and locusts, and was regarded as the farmer's friend.

Most erroneous ideas were held concerning it. Theophrastus called it a precious stone, and Pliny spoke of its medicinal qualities and the employment of it as an article of luxury.

Indians had the same passion for grains of coral as Europeans have since had for pearls. The ancient Gauls ornamented their bucklers and helmets with coral, while the Romans placed pieces of coral on the cradles of new-born infants, to preserve them from infantile maladies ; and Roman physicians prescribed preparations of coral to invalids suffering from fever, fainting-fits and ophthalmia.

Of course coral forms a fruitful source of fairy-tales among the fishermen, some of which are very fascinating, and indeed they should be so ; the dullest imagination must be stimu-lated by a sight of the submarine pictures pre-sented to it when the water is deep and clear ; the extensive coral groves are indeed beautiful, planted as they are in beds of white smooth sand, and showing through the transparent water the various colours of pink, blue, white, and yellow.

There is a very interesting property possessed by coral, which gives it even now the high rank it has always occupied in medicine. It seems that there are people who cannot wear coral against their skin without discolouring it ; as a rule they are invalids who act so curiously on the coral. The ancients declared that if a person wearing a coral necklace was on the verge of an illness, the coral showed discoloration before the person was conscious of the approach of the sickness or disease. Naturalists and chemists have tried to dis-cover the cause of this curious property, but at present there is no solution of it.

---

rly 1000 years B.C.
† *insects found buried in amber are similar to ıh which we are familiar, but the plants are known on the North Sea coast.*

ANSWERS TO CORRESPONDENTS.

EDUCATIONAL.

THE AUTHOR of *The Stocking-Knitting Guide.*—We thank you much for sending us a copy of your most useful Manual which, we are glad to see, is in its third edition (price 6¼d. post free). We are also glad that you have employed the Women's Printing Society, Limited, whose printing does them the greatest credit. We naturally feel a special interest in women's work and new occupations, respecting which we frequently publish articles for the benefit of our girls.

MISS LOUISA BROUGH.—We thank you for your prospectus, and think your institution of a Central Registry for Teachers most valuable (office, 24, Craven Street, Charing Cross, W.C.). For the benefit of our readers we may observe that as Secretary of the Association of Head Mistresses of Endowed and Proprietary Schools, Miss Brough is in constant communication with the heads of the principal public schools for girls throughout the country. She supplies university graduates, trained and certificated teachers for public and private subjects, kindergarten mistresses, and English and foreign governesses for private families. The fees are moderate. Miss Brough has been officially connected with the Women's Education Union, the Teachers' Training Registration Society, the Brompton Evening College for Women, the Teachers' Guild, and the Association of Head Mistresses of Endowed and Proprietary Schools.

BARBARA.—Our English education as established by law, or at least compulsory, dates from the reign of Alfred the Great, who commanded that the son of every freeman, who could afford it, should be taught reading and writing. The earliest Hebrew schools are said to have been established after the Babylonian captivity, by Rabbis, who received children of upwards of six years of age.

DOUBTFUL.—If you be really in earnest and desirous to make yourself well acquainted with the foundation of Christian belief, write for the schemes to the Secretary, 11, Buckingham Street, Strand, W.C., and pay your fee of 1s. The Christian Evidence Society holds both elementary and advanced examinations on Christian Evidence, and gives certificates and prizes of from 10s. to £3. Send a stamped envelope for reply, or call at the office.

HON. SEC., "G. B. C."—We are happy to inform our readers of your newly instituted German Book Club, having already given a notice of your French Postal Library. As there exists a demand for such a society, it was desirable to form one. But we must forewarn our readers that unless they send stamped envelopes for information they cannot expect to obtain it. Girls are too often very thoughtless, and presume on the kindness of those who devote much time and thought to benefit them unremunerated. Address of the Hon. Sec., 15, Vener Road, Sydenham, S.E.

MUSIC.

MINNIE sends some bars of music and requests to know how they are to be played (a passage from "Rondo Brillante," Opera 100, by J. N. Hummel). The notes in the treble are to be played as evenly as possible, notwithstanding their being irregular in number. The directions given in Italian, *i.e.* *L'istesso movimento, ma cantabile assai,* means in the same time, but tolerably singing, *i.e.* bringing out the melody as if in a song. There is no "l" in the word "oblige."

LEONORA LEAR.—1. We could not give you a private opinion as an indisputable fact, so many and great are the diversities of taste amongst persons who may be all equally qualified to entertain an opinion. You do not specify whether you mean composers or instrumental performers, and if the latter, on what instrument—2. Your handwriting is good, and especially so for manuscript writing.

T. D. DERRICK, STROON, and LILL.—Send a stamped envelope to Mrs. H. Rowson, 32, Aldridge Road Villas, Westbourne Park, W., for information respecting her musical society for the circulation of piano pieces and songs. She sends out twelve pieces and twelve songs in the course of the year; and the subscription is 5s. per annum, or half terms at 2s. 6d. Tell her the names of the pieces you can play, and she will know what to send.

MISCELLANEOUS.

LILY HARTLE.—We cannot prescribe for ulcers on the eyeball. Go to an Eye Infirmary for advice.

ELLA ELLIOT.—The fashion in men's slippers seems to incline altogether to leather ones—Turkish and such-like. The old worked ones in Berlin wool cost so much in the making-up, and were dusty likewise, that we are not surprised at their dropping out of fashion. Whoever heard of an intended bride giving no love-token to her *fiancé.* But, naturally, the intrinsic worth of the gift must be regulated by her means. A trifling gift of a lasting nature should suffice, when a girl has little to expend.

N. ANGELOGIE.—We presume that your father is aware of your engagement, and has given his consent. In this case you should make known to him your future husband's wishes, and let him arrange matters for you. Possibly he is not looking for a wife, lest it should deprive you of so comfortable a home as you have hitherto had before you could make one of your own. But under present circumstances he might arrange for a few months' delay of your marriage, so that he might make his own arrangements.

MABELLE.—Some people say that camphorated chalk has a tendency to make the teeth brittle, but certainly not to decay. Exactly the reverse.

A. B. C.—The most Protestant kingdom in the world is that of Sweden and Norway. The national church is Lutheran, and there is a large proportion of Protestant dissenters, such as Baptists and Methodists.

VERUS.—1. September 18th, 1875, was a Saturday.—2. The name Lavinia is Latin, and signifies "of *Latium.*"

MARIE ANTOINETTE.—1. August 20th, 1877, was a Monday.—2. The story called "A Daughter named Damaris," is in vol. iii. It is in too many parts to be named by the pages.

"LOVE IN A PUZZLE."—It would not only be "unladylike" for a girl of only seventeen, or of any age, to "show symptoms of love" for a man, but it would be grossly indelicate, unless he were her affianced husband. When a girl meets a man of her acquaintance, she may bow to him with a slight smile, or avoid seeing him, but not so as to pass him rudely and ignore his presence. The man can only raise his hat if she bow to him; a recognition rests entirely with herself. No man may thus claim acquaintance with her, excepting with her consent.

LENE AVE.—Plum-porridge and plum-pudding were served with the first course of a Christmas dinner in old times. It is named by Sir Roger de Coverley and in "Poor Robin's Almanack" for 1750, as elsewhere. A recipe for a pudding much resembling our national institution for Christmas fare is given by Rabisha, in the *Whole Body of Cookery Dissected* (1675), which was to be boiled in a basin. Probably, as being a universal favourite, it was selected for our great festival; and Mrs. Frazer, "sole teacher of the art of cookery" in Edinburgh, and our earliest known authority on the art, describes its concoction under the name "plumb-pudding."

HERALDRY.—No, everybody has not got a coat-of-arms. They are hereditary distinctions, belonging to the ancient lords of the soil and to persons who have had them conferred on them for gallant deeds of arms by the sovereign in the olden times. Many persons in a good position at present have risen from the middle, and even lower classes, and have purchased new ones—that have never belonged to their families—by paying the fees due to the College of Heralds, for making a coat and a crest. All the ancient families of the nobility were knights, and bore arms, shields, and helmets (the crests upon them). And as armour is no longer worn these insignia are represented on their plate, seals, etc., to record their hereditary honours and deeds of valour by arms. Money can now obtain escutcheons; but, of course, they are of no historic interest.

SE VAINCRE POUR AIMER.—An English girl of the upper class cannot walk alone in the fields, unless they belong to her family and are near her home also; and it would be quite unsuitable for her to ride alone on a bicycle. A foreigner should certainly be accompanied by a chaperon when she visits England. It is not desirable for a girl to send presents to young men; it is only done by girls of a lower class.

STELLA.—You are only a minor, and too young to take any step in life for yourself. It is your parents' place to find a suitable situation for you, and make all needful arrangements for placing you in it. It is not your business to select the office or firm and to make terms with them. It should be seen that you are under the protection of your father.

KATHLEEN.—We know nothing of the society which you say is sending old stamps to China. Inquire of the person who named the society to you.

JENNY GIRL, "What are 'wonders'?" We have no idea, and can give no recipe, and must humbly take rank with the wondering "Twinkle, twinkle little Star" girl.

A SHY YOUNG PUSS should try benzine for the grease spots. It can be obtained in small quantities at the old shops, but must be carefully used and stored away from the chance of accident by fire.

ELSIE KRINKE.—What a monstrous idea you have communicated to us, and that after all we have said on the subject: "Might a girl of sixteen look out for a young gentleman to make herself especially pleasant to?" No womanmanship, or old-e who had any delicacy and self-respect would degrade herself by "looking out for a man!" As to a girl of a girl, who ought to be learning her lessons in the schoolroom, and has scarcely laid aside her dolls, proposing to pay her addresses to a man, it is simply disgusting.

www.ingramcontent.com/pod-product-compliance
Lightning Source LLC
Chambersburg PA
CBHW021643270326
41931CB00008B/1141